Tomorrow

LEARNING AMHARIC THROUGH STORY

Tomorrow

LEARNING AMHARIC THROUGH STORY

GLOSSAHOUSE MODERN LANGUAGES SERIES
VOLUME 2

SERIES EDITOR
T. Michael W. Halcomb

AUTHOR
T. Michael W. Halcomb

GlossaHouse
Wilmore, KY
GlossaHouse.com

Tomorrow : Learning Amharic Through Story

Publisher's Cataloging-in-Publication Data

Tomorrow: Learning Amharic Through Story. Amharic.

Halcomb, T. Michael W.
  Tomorrow : Learning Amharic Through Story / T. Michael W. Halcomb. – Wilmore, KY : GlossaHouse, ©2018.

        viii, 135 pages ; cm. -- (GlossaHouse modern language series)

        ISBN-13: 9781942697718 (paperback)

        1. Amharic language--Textbooks for foreign speakers--English. 2. Amharic language--Composition and exercises. I. Title. II. Series.

Library of Congress Control Number: 2018945242

Fonts used to create the front matter are available at Linguistsoftware.com/lgku.html; and, text layout, cover design, and book design are by T. Michael W. Halcomb.

This book is dedicated to Abdi, Abdissa, Genet, Elias, Yared, Mengi, Nebiat, and Tekabe—those who helped me fight the good fight and finish the race.

And to Sara, whose smile still warms me and whose words still haunt me. If ever you read this, know that I tried. And know that I think about you often and will continue to until the end of my days. Oh, how I wish you could have come, too.

And may Duni Zenaye and her mom, along with Zaid Tesfaye, Membera the robber of orphans, and Almaz the corrupt chief, all reap the fruits of their injustices.

GLOSSAHOUSE MODERN LANGUAGE SERIES

The goal of the GlossaHouse Modern Language Series is to facilitate the creation and publication of innovative, affordable, and accessible scholarly resources, whether print or digital, that advance learning and research in the areas of modern texts and languages.

TABLE OF CONTENTS

Tomorrow

Tomorrow: The Story of this Book

Focal Words: Tomorrow (ነገ: nEh-geh) | Adoption (ጉዲፈቻ: gu-di-fAh-chah) | No! (አይ: Aye) | Alphabet (ፊደል: fEE-dehl)

The word "tomorrow" (ነገ: nEh-geh) is one that, more than any other, captured the essence of my recent experiences in Ethiopia (June-August and October-November of 2017). On the morning of Monday, July 26th, my wife and I received an email from our adoption agency. That email suggested that we might want to consider traveling to Addis in order to try to make progress on our adoption (ጉዲፈቻ: gu-di-fAh-chah). On the one hand, since we had been in the process for five long years, this seemed a bit hopeful. One the other hand, since it was on our dime and since we were in the midst of a major family move, the timing wasn't the best. But we talked and I decided, "I'll go tomorrow."

So, within a few hours of that email, I booked a one-way ticket to Ethiopia. I packed my bags, got a few things in order, and flew out on Tuesday morning. When I arrived on Wednesday morning, I stepped off the plane and hit the ground running. For the next seven weeks I found myself in a vortex of highs and lows. There were days of victory and days of nothing. There were moments of pure beauty and utter hardship. After telling my friend, John Hobbins, about my first week, he said my stories teetered between "the harrowing and the heartwarming." That was a very apt description!

But the title of this book doesn't simply refer to my quick-to-book-a-flight attitude. There are yet other nuances to the word "tomorrow." This term, for example, encompasses the mentality of our Ethiopian caseworker, whom I shall refer to here as Gez. When I had visited Ethiopia ten months prior, I took to Gez right away. He was kind and seemed to be in this for all the right reasons.

He told my wife and me that he was doing this work for the glory of God. This time, however, he distinctly said that this job was for his flesh—to take care of himself. And during my time there, that became increasingly apparent as the days went by.

Literally, every time I tried to get Gez to file some paper, deliver some piece of paperwork, meet somewhere, etc., his response was always, "Tomorrow!" There are more than a few Ethiopians, especially those of this generation, who will quickly admit that this is the mindset ingrained in the culture at large. And this is why, in so many domains, Ethiopia seems so inefficient. I and another friend, John Walters, who was a travel mate during many of these days, often referred to the root of this as "The Four Cs: Corruption, Callousness, Carelessness, and Chaos."

I think there is much truth to that. Indeed, many Ethiopians are very up front about such things, ready and willing to talk about government corruption and all of the madness, hardship, and cruelty that often results from it. In a conversation with a hotel manager, Stephanos (one of the few guys with a Greek rather than Semitic name), I asked him, a man in his twenties, if he thought things would ever change. Without a blink, he insisted, "No!" (አይ: Aye) And then asked, "How can they?" In that vein, too, "tomorrow" carries meaning. It's a word lacking hope.

I went to Ethiopia to adopt two little ones. My heart's desire was the same this time as it was eight years ago when I adopted my first son: to give these two a better "tomorrow." I want them to have chances. I want them to be able to seize opportunities. I want them to be able to be change agents. If I can do that, then maybe that's how things can change. Maybe. Either way, it is certainly heartbreaking to hear this young man, full of talent and promise, remark that his future is limited, that his "tomorrow" has predefined bookends.

I write this book, then, with these nuances in mind. I do, indeed, tell stories of the harrowing and heartwarming. I share, of course, from my limited perspective. I know that and know it well. But it is a perspective that, for some, might help capture what life here seems to be like for a handful of different people—some whom I tell multiple stories about. Please, allow their stories to intersect with your own. Because I believe when that happens, you're likely to wake up a better and more informed person tomorrow.

And also, please allow the popular language, Amharic, to intersect with your own. I have worked hard to attempt to include terms that I view as survival words and phrases. These are bits of the language or "Focal Words," that I found myself hearing and using (or at least trying to use) over and over again. The sort of approach I employ here to gain familiarity with the language, what I call a "narrative domains" approach, is somewhat innovative. I believe that, in addition to consulting a dictionary or grammar, for instance, it is an effective path into the language. Read each story in this book a few times if you need to in order to let the words soak in, in order to internalize them.

I have purposefully attempted to limit the number of words I introduce in a section to three to five. Hopefully, this will prevent information overload. The terms are found at the beginning, middle, and end of each story. There are also several "Vocabulary Review" sections across the entirety of the book that cover the nearly three hundred words. If needed, I've included all the Amharic words found throughout the book in an index. As in the review sections, there they are also arranged alphabetically by English. The Amharic script immediately follows. A transliteration (i.e. a letter-for-letter equivalent or approximation) comes after that, which helps readers pronounce the words. In some words, you'll notice that certain vowels are capitalized. Note that this is where the stress falls within the Amharic term being pronounced.

Additionally, at the end of each story, if you have an interest in attempting to go deeper with the language, you are encouraged to compose a paragraph-length story (3-5 sentences) and drop in the Amharic words, script and all, where they might fit. In other words, in the "Your Turn" sections, allow these vocabulary words to connect in a way that forms a unique narrative. This story will, in turn, reinforce links in the narrative domain that you initially encountered. It will, moreover, give you practice writing the script and, as such, help you further internalize the language.

I would also encourage you to then read the story aloud and record yourself doing so. This gives you a chance at pronunciation and hearing the word. To sharpen your skills, listen to the recording as many times as you need to, consistently reinforcing the narrative domain connections. I, likewise, hope to provide audio companion files for this work that will be available for purchase and download in the near future. If you have an interest in purchasing those when they come available, check out www.GlossaHouse.com. There is also a pronunciation guide provided in the very back of the book. For a fuller description and understanding of the alphabet (ፊደል: fEE-dehl), see my book *Introducing Amharic* (GlossaHouse, 2015). As there, I have tried to be creative here in my approach to teaching the language. In addition, see my 2016 thesis completed at the University of Kentucky titled "Generating Amharic Present Tense Verbs: A Network Morphology & DATR Account." (Google it!)

Hopefully, my strategy here will aid you in gaining more familiarity with Amharic in terms of both speaking and reading. This book, then, is meant to be educational in at least a couple different ways. As noted just above, one hope is that you'll grow in your knowledge and use of Amharic. Another hope, also already stated, is that you will hear some of these stories and find them thought-provoking. Perhaps you'll even be prompted to take action. And maybe there are other affects this book will have that I simply cannot foresee. Whatever the result, I can only hope that this book makes you a better, more aware person. May it be!

Focal Words: Tomorrow (ነገ: nEh-geh) | Adoption (ጉዲፋቻ: gu-di-fAh-chah) | No! (አይ: Aye) | Alphabet (ፊደል: fEE-dehl)

Your Turn: Using the space below or an additional piece of paper, compose an original paragraph in your native language and, as you do, insert each of the "Focal Words" from the preceding story.

Adult Orphan

Focal Words: Children (ልጆች: lee-jOh-ch) | World (ዓለም: Ah-lehm) |
God (እግዚአብሔር: ig-zAhb-heyr)

The word orphan bothers me. I don't like it. In fact, I hate it.
I wish there were no such word in the English language or in any
language. In Amharic, there actually isn't a single word; it takes
multiple words that, when put together, convey the idea of "orphan."
But I simply despise what the word "orphan" stands for. That's
because there is no orphan, not a single one, whose circumstances
did not arise from brokenness and hardship. That's a fact. If the
blood of the martyrs is the seed of the church, then perhaps the
brokenness of this world is the seed of the world orphan crisis.

It is this crisis that has changed my life. I think about that
often, especially when I'm in Ethiopia. This place is hard. It can be
very unforgiving. But the fact is not lost on me, not even for a
second, that, while Ethiopia has created some of the most painful
experiences I've ever had, it has also given me three of the greatest
gifts of my life—my children (ልጆች: lee-jOh-ch).

Three of my four children, that is, the three born in Ethiopia,
have all lived in orphanages at some point in their young lives. I will
refrain from explaining to you the dire circumstances of their
situations here, but I will say that none of them had it easy. None of
them had it comfortable. None of them had it anywhere close to
what would be acceptable in a developed country.

Yet, as I look at them, I marvel. These kids, they are strong—
very strong. Sure, I had my fair share of hardships growing up, many
of us have but, for me, none like this. As a child, I never spent time
under the roof of an orphanage. As an adult, however, I've spent
many hours in such places. Places most of the world (ዓለም: Ah-
lehm) would never care to venture and never will.

It wasn't until recently, however, that I realized I was an
adult orphan. I've not had contact with either of my parents in over a
decade. Circumstances don't permit it and, even if they did, I'm not

sure it could or would or even should work. That, too, is a broken relationship. It's severely broken and irreparable.

And but for the love and grace of God (እግዚአብሔር: ig-zAhb-heyr) in my own life, I surely cannot pinpoint why things are different. When I hold my kids in these orphanages, all I want is to get them out of there. I want to see their personalities full-on blossom. I want to play with them, hug them, and kiss them without the oversight of some gate guard who seemingly couldn't care less.

But sometimes, when I leave the orphanage at the end of the day, questions flood my mind. Questions like, "How could any dad walk out on his children and the mother of his children?" And "How could any mother do the same?" And "How could any parent possibly inflict abuse on these innocent little ones who are just aching to be loved?" And "How could any parent wish ill upon their children?" None of that makes any sense to me.

Obviously, I do not mean to imply that all orphans are in orphanages because of the limited set of circumstances I mentioned above. Not at all! Sometimes parents have little to do with it. Fatal accidents, acts of nature, kidnapping and trafficking, etc., often give rise to such circumstances. Nevertheless, the questions raised a moment ago describe very real situations for many, myself included.

And so, as I sit in a hotel room now in Ethiopia and reflect on the fact that I'm an adult orphan and that three of my children were, at one time or another, orphans, it only strengthens my resolve to continue trying to put a tiny dent in the problem. And it reminds me of that verse in the Gospel of Mark where Jesus says to Judas, "You will always have the poor among you, but you will not always have me." Many read that as if Jesus were making a timeless statement, proclaiming a timeless truth—one that suggests we must all just resign ourselves to the fact that poverty will always exist. Or, to use that as a parallel analogy, that the orphan crisis will always exist.

But that's not what Jesus was saying. Rather, he was calling Judas to the floor, calling him to account. He was outing him for, at one and the same time, stealing money from the ministry purse yet cursing a woman intending to help Jesus. In other words, Jesus was touching the raw nerve of Judas's hypocrisy and greed. And in that, Jesus was saying, "You're right Judas, as long as there are greedy people like you, this crap will always exist." And there's the timely truth: As long as we're greedy, nothing will change. That's the point!

Many of the orphans here in Ethiopia would not be so were it not for greed, greed by government officials, greedy hands of adoption agents, and greed coursing through the veins of mothers and fathers. In just the last two weeks, the previous orphanage director where my daughter has been for the last year-and-a-half, has fled the country along with her boss, a former government official, named Zaid. They were tipped off that they were under investigation or, more aptly put, that their greed had finally caught up to them.

They were a couple of modern-day Judas's stealing from the ministry pot, but this time literally stealing from the mouths and bellies of babies and children. Any vengeful cell in my body seems to hope that there's a special corner in hell for such people, those who are creators and progenitors of this vicious cycle of brokenness. If that's the case, then I am left to sit here wondering what it'll be like. Will they spend that next lifetime reaping their own gross reward: being orphans in the darkness of hell? If I'm completely honest, I'm not so sure that bothers me, for it's an orphan crisis of a different sort altogether. I'm just glad I can leave such vengeance to the Lord.

Focal Words: Children (ልጆች: lee-jOh-ch) | World (ዓለም: Ah-lehm) | God (እግዚአብሔር: ig-zAhb-heyr)

Your Turn:

Retarded Plankton

Focal Words: Roundabout (አደባባይ: ah-deh-bAh-bay) | Friend (ጓደኛ: gwah-dEh-nyah) | Garbage Dump (ቆሻ: qOh-shay)

    In the West, the word "retarded" has, for all intents and purposes, fallen out of use. Social stigmas attached to this word are certainly the cause of that. I grew up hearing the term often, even used for two of my own uncles, who suffered mental and physical disabilities. Up until July 8th, 2017, were you to for ask me, for some odd reason, the last time I heard that term used, I wouldn't have been able to tell you. Were you to ask me today, however, that's the date I would point you to.

    On that particular day, I was sitting in Hard Rock Café in Addis Ababa. It's located on the fourth floor of Gollagul Tower, which stands on a busy city roundabout (አደባባይ: ah-deh-bAh-bay). Throughout the restaurant, several televisions line the walls. A day before, during the G20 Summit in Hamburg, Germany, Donald Trump and Vladimir Putin had met for the first time. All of the televisions were semi-frozen and kind of jittery with the image of the infamous first handshake between the two world leaders.

    One side of the restaurant, however, was all windows. Along with my friend (ጓደኛ: gwah-dEh-nyah), John, we buoyed up to a table near the glass and looked out over the city. A little girl wearing a pink jacket was holding her mom's hand as they ventured across the zebra striped crosswalk. She was treating the painted white lines as if they were stepping stones, making her best effort to hop across.

    Not infrequently, cow herders and donkey drivers, walking right in the midst of buses, motorcycles, taxis, and cars, were guiding flocks across the roundabout. Pedestrians, as is typical in the city, were, for the most part, ignoring the crosswalks and venturing right out into the middle of traffic.

    It goes without saying that those walking have the right away, but it either takes some intense nerve or sheer carelessness to step out in front of an onslaught of oncoming traffic. Kids do it. The elderly do it. Animals do it. Police do it. It's common. An unspoken rule, I guess, that one learns in time.

John and I ordered personal pizzas. He's something of an adventurous eater. I'm not. I went for the pineapple and cheese pizza while he got the loaded type. As we were eating, we marveled at those continually braving danger down in the street below. At one point, I directed his attention to an area of rather green grass in the middle of the roundabout. It was divided into a grid of sorts.

All of the plots were finished...except one. All of the squares in the grid had green grass...except one. That odd-one-out was just filled with trash; it had become a small garbage dump (ቆሽ: qOh-shay). In many ways, it blended right in with the rest of the city, with its surroundings. Yet, in another way, it stood out like a sore thumb or, better yet, an eyesore. The plastic bags, the drink bottles, and everything else that was in it caught my attention.

John proceeded to talk about how, on an island where he lived, trash like that would just float to shore all the time. He talked about how it littered the beaches. And he talked about how it was damaging the plankton, effectually retarding it. The scientists, he said, were now frequently talking about retarded plankton and its role in the surrounding ecosystem. So, there we were, two guys eating our pizza and watching donkeys in the roundabout, talking about retarded plankton. It was a Saturday.

When you run yourself ragged every weekday trying to get adoption paperwork completed and trying to love on your kids as much as you can, and when you can't do that on the weekend because the government essentially stops, which stops you, I guess that's what you do. You talk about retarded plankton. It helps pass the time.

Focal Words: Roundabout (አደባባይ: ah-deh-bAh-bay) | Friend (ጓደኛ: gwah-dEh-nyah) | Garbage Dump (ቆሽ: qOh-shay)

Your Turn:

Running in the Rain

Focal Words: Rainy Season (ክረምት: keh-rImt) | Rain (ዝናብ: zEh-nahb) | Coffee (ቡና: bU-nah)

Many of the people we encounter in life mean nothing to us. They are not a friend, family member, co-worker, or teammate, but only a stranger. Yet, these strangers are everywhere. They surround us. We walk past them at the market, pump gas next to them at the gas station, and sit near them in restaurants.

But my time in Ethiopia reminds me that these "stranger encounters" are often great gifts. Sometimes the gifts are small but sometimes large. Sometimes they are insignificant but sometimes incalculable. And sometimes they just leave you thinking, imagining what that person's life must be like.

I met a stranger in Afen Jober, a sub-city of Addis. This stranger was like that—he left me wondering. I met him during Kerimt (ክረምት: keh-rImt), that time of the year Ethiopians refer to as "Rainy Season." During this season, the downpours of rain (ዝናብ: zEh-nahb) are often quite erratic. They're powerful, too. Typically, they last for 30-40 minutes. Sometimes there's hail, sometimes there's lightning, and pretty often there's a power outage.

One day, while standing under the sheet metal roof of a 5x5 food shop in Afen Jober, I watched one of these storms roll in and then out. This one only lasted fifteen minutes. Under the roof with me was a little guy named Habtam, must've only been 6 or 7 years old. His Amharic was definitely better than mine and, if we were keeping score, I'd probably say his English was better than my Amharic, too.

I asked him his name and how he was doing. He tried to speak some Amharic to me but I didn't quite understand. I had a green rain jacket on and he had a long-sleeved t-shirt. After attempting to make very short conversation, the guy running the little shop handed him a bag. All I could gather was that he had purchased coffee (ቡና: bU-nah), likely for his mother.

10

Once the shopkeeper handed him the little black plastic bag, he looked up at me, looked out at the rain, and started rocking back and forth like track stars do as they first take stance in their blocks. Then, also like them, he suddenly froze. He looked at me once more, turned his head to the sky, looked both ways, and darted out into the road. He had the form of a runner. It was natural.

His fists were clinched, one holding tightly to the bag, his arms at ninety-degree angles, and his head was up. He was booking it. He left me no time to say goodbye. Perhaps our eyes or our body language conveyed that. In no time, though, he was running like a star…in a pair of crocs. That takes talent.

As he peeled off into the rainy distance, I tried to watch where he was going. When he rounded the bend and disappeared behind a fence, which like many things in Addis, was also made of sheet metal, I lost track of him. Beyond being impressed by his great running capabilities, I marveled at his determination to get to the store, in the middle of a downpour, and get home as soon as possible.

I stood and waited for the rain to finish. It did, just three or four minutes after Habtam bolted out of the blocks. But he wasn't waiting. Maybe he was in a hurry. Maybe his delivery was urgent. Or maybe, like most kids, he just wanted to play in the rain. Regardless, I stepped out from under that sheet metal roof thanking God for that moment—a gift.

Focal Words: Rainy Season (ክረምት: keh-rImt) | Rain (ዝናብ: zEh-nahb) | Coffee (ቡና: bU-nah)

Your Turn:

That's the Ticket

Focal Words: Ethiopia (ኢትዮጵያ: eet-yO-pee-ya) | Car (መኪና: meh-kEE-nah) | Police (ፖሊስ: po-lEEs)

To many Westerners, Ethiopia (ኢትዮጵያ: eet-yO-pee-ya) has long been known as a place of struggle. The famines and utter destitution that many have seen clips of on television are certainly part of the reason for this. I grew up seeing commercials for a well-known children's fund in Ethiopia. In those commercials kids were often shown with flies crawling on their faces, dilapidated homes were nearly always the backdrop, and there were malnourished babies with wholly visible rib cages. These featured prominently.

It's tough to admit but, all these years later, those things still exist. Hunger is still a major force to be reckoned with in Ethiopia. All over the country's capital city, Addis Ababa, beggars line the sidewalks in hopes of receiving some sort of help. In America, street corner beggars are not an uncommon sight. The "Will Work for Food" sign has almost become as iconic as the Golden Arches. The city where I currently live, in fact, just implemented a van service to go around and pick these individuals up, offering them $10/hr jobs on the spot. That, however, didn't quite appeal to many of them, so, they kept doing their thing.

But, at least with regard to where I'm from in the States, there's one major difference when it comes to beggars: age. In Addis those looking for help from the sidewalk or street corner span the entire spectrum—baby to elder. And all day thousands upon thousands of people drive and walk past them. Sometimes they help and sometimes they don't.

One day, while stopped at one of the few red lights in the entire city, I decided I wanted to help. I had just eaten lunch at a restaurant and decided against throwing quite a bit of extra food away. So, I asked for a "takeaway" box, as they call them in Ethiopia. After they put the two pancakes in, I left. On this particular day, I saw a mother and three little children sitting in the rain on a mud-laden sidewalk. My heart ached for them and, so, I opened my car door, crossed two empty lanes, stepped up onto the sidewalk and handed this mother and her kids the food. I was compelled to do this and I'm not sure anything could've stopped me.

But in the short amount of time it took to do that, the two lanes had filled up. So, as is common in Addis, I did a little weaving through the stopped traffic and made my way back to my car (መኪና: meh-kEE-nah). As I was getting in, one of the traffic police (ፖሊስ: po-lEEs) approached and proceeded to give my driver a ticket. Why? Because I exited the car (to help someone in need)! Now, in Addis, people cut through the streets all the time totally ignoring the crosswalks. That's just how it is. I'm nearly convinced that Ethiopians have a sixth sense for this sort of thing.

Well, immediately after receiving the ticket, a guy in the cab just to my right, a native Ethiopian, began screaming at me. He yelled, "This is Ethiopia! Here, red light means stop! This is Ethiopia! Do you understand?!" He also sprinkled a couple f-bombs in there. I was a bit shell-shocked. In this land, where people constantly walk out into traffic and where beggars line the sidewalks because there is no other option, I both received a ticket and a good ol' cussin', as we might say in Kentucky.

In that instance, the saying "No good deed goes unpunished" came to mind. I'd be lying, however, if I told you that was the first and only time a good deed of mine in Ethiopia reaped the reward of a punishment. Unfortunately, I'm not a liar. I'm just telling the truth—quite like those commercials I grew up seeing. The only difference is, now I have some first-hand insight into some of the reasons why things likely haven't changed.

Focal Words: Ethiopia (ኢትዮጵያ: eet-yO-pee-ya) | Car (መኪና: meh-kEE-nah) | Police (ፖሊስ: po-lEEs)

Your Turn:

God's Timing?

Focal Words: America (አሜሪካ: ah-mEh-ree-kah) | injera (እንጀራ: in-jEh-rah) | Bible (መጽሐፍ ቅዱስ: mEts'-haf qih-dUs)

In America, clichés abound in Christian circles. Pastors love them. Churchgoers and pew-sitters love them. Authors who tag the label "Christian" on to their books love them. Parody shirt makers love them. Indeed, clichés are a beloved thing, a type of golden calf. That's why I hate them; nay, I despise them. The unceasing attempts to boil the Christian walk down into seemingly digestible maxims is, from my vantage point, terribly problematic.

In fact, many times these corny sayings end up being hurtful. That's because, in the first place, they are often thoughtless, emotionless, and ill-founded. The one that may well irk me the most is: "God's timing." This phrase seems to be used without end amongst those in the adoption process. When paperwork takes years to file and adoption agents are too lazy or ill-equipped to help make it happen, they simply step back and tell parents, "Just be patient, it's all in God's timing."

What a stupid remark! I heard the same thing while sitting in federal government building known as MOWA. This is actually short for The Ministry of Women's, Children's, and Youth Affairs. It was a Monday near the end of July and I had been sitting there for nearly four or five hours when, in comes a woman from America (አሜሪካ: ah-mEh-ree-kah) who, because she was adopting, also needed some paperwork to be finalized. After making some small talk and discussing our cases, she pulled the God's timing card on me saying, "Just be positive. All positive vibes today. It's all in God's timing."

Without missing a beat and without hesitation, I replied, "Well, I'm sorry, but I don't believe in the notion of God's timing." Judging by the look on her face, you would have thought she might have eaten some bad injera (እንጀራ: in-jEh-rah), a local Ethiopian cuisine, the night before.

14

I commented further, "If this is all about God's timing, then I think he's doing a pretty bad job. I'm sorry, I'm just not there with you theologically." With the type of arrogance so commonly found in Americans, she said while laughing and shaking her head, "Theologically. Ha. Theologically." Needless to say, that was the end of the conversation with her. It was abundantly clear that she lacked both the intellectual depth to continue on with the conversation and the capacity to have her neatly packaged and cliché-based views challenged.

Dear reader, I would like to ask you one favor: Never resort to chalking someone's pains, hurts, struggles, and frustrations up to "God's timing." That's a coward's way out and it's not at all helpful. Instead, it is simply the offer of a cold answer to someone who is likely in need of a warm hug and presence. I mean, just stop and think about it for a moment. In the Bible (መጽሐፍ ቅዱስ: mEts'-haf qih-dUs), there is no concept or doctrine that suggests that God is operating on a different timeline. Rather, God is portrayed, from the beginning, as the one who created time and, as the story goes, stepped into it in the form of a man.

Sure, God is eternal, but that has more to do with his nature and attributes than anything. Moreover, when one resorts to the "God's timing" remark, they are, whether knowingly or not, doing two things: 1) Putting up a spiritual front because saying things like that makes them appear spiritual, and 2) Suggesting that God has wants and that those wants are pinpointed on a predetermined timeline and, if you get lucky or pray hard enough or are good enough, maybe you'll be fortunate enough to see such things transpire. And, if you do, you will once again appear spiritual because things went right for you.

I'm calling that bluff though. Such views are a sham and, while they may earn folks some spiritual street cred in some circles, they do not in mine. Indeed, such views when considered in the face of all this world's evil, ultimately result in the worship of a tyrant God.

Seriously, what type of God "wants" there to be orphans? And what type of God "wants" them to be in and/or remain in horrendous situations when they have an out? To pin such things on to the God of the Bible is blasphemous and heretical. But that's what is happening when someone tells me that God has a time in which his wants will be fulfilled, including the want to hold my child hostage in a situation of hurt, unsanitariness, loneliness, hunger, lack of education, and the like.

That's not the God I read about in the Bible, the God who created time and acts in time and calls his people to do the same. It is God who fights for the poor and needy and calls his people to do the same; the God for whom the purest form of religion is looking after widows and orphans; the God who gets pissed off when people attempt to thwart little ones from coming to him; the God who views righteous anger as a form of holiness; the God who never sleeps; and, the God who is love and who remains at work in time, the very time he created and set in motion, and is continually inviting us to join him. That's the God I read about.

So, I think it's about time we let that old cliché die. And when we do, we shall look anew for the beauty of God that is present in us and around us, that is moving and bidding us to join him. And once we join in, once we're hard at work, perhaps the propensity to chalk things up to un-Christian and un-biblical sayings won't be so potent or readily available. Perhaps, in time, bad habits such as these will vanish. I sure hope so...in time.

Focal Words: America (አሜሪካ: ah-mEh-ree-kah) | injera (እንጀራ: in-jEh-rah) | Bible (መጽሐፍ ቅዱስ: mEts'-haf qih-dUs)

Your Turn:

Bonding Over Smuggled Pizza

Focal Words: Daughter (ሴት ልጅ: sAyt lihj) | Food (ምግብ: mAh-gihb) | Beautiful (ቆንጆ: qOhn-joh) | Dad (አባባ: ah-bAh-bah)

There are three times in my life, all in my youth, that I can distinctly remember stealing something. Once was a piece of candy from a gas station, once a cassette tape from a theme park, and once a cassette tape from a big box store. What I have no recollection of prior to my most recent trip to Ethiopia, however, is smuggling something into a place. Now, that sounds a bit more sinister than it really is, so, let me explain.

What I was smuggling in was pizza. The place I was smuggling it into was an orphanage. The reason I was smuggling it in was because my daughter (ሴት ልጅ: sAyt lihj), after I did it the first time, repeatedly asked me to. And when your child is hungry and you are forced to leave them in an Ethiopian orphanage night after night, you don't think twice about doing it.

But other than the fact that her tummy was getting full from the numerous pizzas I managed to sneak in under the radar time and again, this act built a bond between us. This little girl knew that she could trust me. And she knew that she could ask me for things. And she also knew that she effectively had me wrapped around her finger and that I'd do anything she asked. And, perhaps best of all, she knew that we could keep a secret together. As a result, early in my relationship with my daughter, we bonded over smuggled pizza.

I remember the first time I snuck it in. It was wrapped in aluminum foil and I had it stowed in my backpack. There were four pieces. When I showed it to her, she had no idea what it was because she had never seen pizza before. But when I explained to her that it was food (ምግብ: mAh-gihb) and that she should eat it, she shook her head no, got up, and ran off. I was bewildered. I stayed put and, within a couple of minutes, she brought some friends back and shared it with them.

It was actually quite hilarious to watch these little Ethiopian girls eat pizza for the first time. They sat in the dirt, right front of an old rickety swing set, and dove right in. One of them ate it upside down, another picked the cheese off and then licked the sauce off and didn't know what to do with the leftover crust. And another pulled it apart and balled it up into bites as if she were eating injera. In the midst of this wonderful moment, I found myself cracking up.

Yet, I was blown away by my beautiful (ቆንጆ: qOhn-joh) little daughter's selfless attitude time and time again. Never would she would eat the smuggled-in pizza unless her other hungry friends could get in on the action, too. Indeed, every single time that I smuggled pizza in, she would never eat it alone—she always invited others to partake, to share in the experience. In seeing that, I was not only a proud dad (አባባ: ah-bAh-bah) who was extremely proud of his daughter, but I was just proud to be a human witnessing this—seeing a child in rather dire circumstances with the mental wherewithal to share and put others first. Next time you're having a pie, keep that in mind. I will.

Focal Words: Daughter (ሴት ልጅ: sAyt lihj) | Food (ምግብ: mAh-gihb) | Beautiful (ቆንጆ: qOhn-joh) | Dad (አባባ: ah-bAh-bah)

Your Turn:

Arega

Focal Words: Man (ወንድ: wEhnd) | Mother (እናት: Ih-naht) | Money (ብር: bIrr) | Water (ውሃ: wU-ha)

It's one thing to walk into an orphanage and see a bunch of kids already there. It's a completely different thing, however, to sit in the presence of a man (ወንድ: wEhnd), a dad, who, while cradling his daughter in his arms, is in the act of asking the government to place his daughter in one. As you might imagine, that's no easy moment to sit through. It's a gut-wrenching experience, completely heart-breaking.

Truth be told, on most days it would be easy to look down upon such a man. It would be easy to attribute the status of a coward to him. But in this particular instance, that was the farthest thing from my mind. This man was no coward.

His name was Arega. His daughter's name was Habtam. They were from outside Addis, living in the Amhara countryside. Little Habtam was probably 8-years old but because of medical issues, was unable to stand and could barely even hold her neck up. Tired of having to deal with the struggle of raising Habtam, her mother (እናት: Ih-naht) ran out on her and her father. Arega had no idea where she was and, being a rather poor man, simply lacked the necessary means to care for his daughter on his own.

On this day, which seemed especially prone to sporadic and powerful downpours, Arega was drenched. He wore an old khaki-colored jacket with a dingy brown sweater underneath, blue sweat pants with a white line down each side, and blue Crocs. Most certainly, this guy wasn't attempting to keep up appearances; in fact, he was quite the open book.

With the aid of a non-professional translator helping navigate the conversation, I was able to learn a bit about his story. Arega was pleading with the government to keep his daughter close, to place her in an orphanage near him so he could still see her and be part of her life. That's not the type of move a coward or deadbeat makes!

No, one could tell right away that this was a good man. This was a man who stood up in the face of his crappy circumstances to defy the odds. Many American dads would do well to learn from his example. Many dads leave in situations much easier than this and never so much as utter a word to their children. That's a very sad truth!

But Arega, he's one of the good ones. This man was open to sharing and, I must say, it was one of the few times in my life where the depth and height of my compassion for another grown man could hardly be matched. After rubbing his daughter's head, and gently caressing her cheek with the back of my pointer finger in an attempt to calm her down, I and a friend gave him some birr (ብር: bIrr), the local Ethiopian currency, and some water (ውሃ: wU-ha). And just like that, his paperwork was finalized and he was told to follow the government officials aiding him.

I doubt I will ever see Arega or Habtam again. Who knows? Yet, I am forever marked by this brief encounter. For, it taught me many things that I am grateful for, not the least of which is how deep a father's love can go for his child. May the Lord bless these two.

Focal Words: Man (ወንድ: wEhnd) | Mother (እናት: Ih-naht) | Money (ብር: bIrr) | Water (ውሃ: wU-ha)

Your Turn:

Push & Shove

Focal Words: Road (መንገድ: mEhn-gehd) | City (ከተማ: keh-tEh-mah) | Ethiopian (ሐበሻ: hAh-beh-shah) | (White) Foreigner (ፈረንጅ: feh-rIhnj)

If you're a person who likes bartering, downtown Addis is the place to be. Actually, street salesmen line just about every road (መንገድ: mEhn-gehd) and sidewalk throughout the city (ከተማ: keh-tEh-mah). There seems to be a concentrated effort, however, in the city center.

It is not at all uncommon to be sitting in traffic and have a beggar or salesperson come right up to your car and stick their head or hands through your window. These sellers have a persistent push about them. They are relentless. While I actually enjoy the back-and-forth of bartering, on my most recent trip I only fell prey to it once. I bought a poster of the Amharic alphabet, which the guy started at 500 birr and eventually dropped to 50.

One Friday, though, while walking through downtown, a guy approached me and was trying his hardest to get me to buy an Ethiopian magazine. Other than the fact that it looked terribly used and like it might have been published in the 1980s, I just wasn't interested. Sensing that, his push grew more aggressive. For a minute or two, he walked right alongside me. His friend eventually joined him and, in fact, a third fellow, his boss, was trailing behind.

At one point, he started to stick his hand down my pant pocket. While I am not an aggressive guy, that kind of sent me over the edge. I grabbed his hand and his arm and with as much force as I could, shoved him away. He stumbled back a bit and, before I knew it, the three guys were together, staring me down and raising their voices at me. They were acting as if I had done something wrong.

It was a moment of infuriation for me. Personally, I've never seen an Ethiopian (ሐበሻ: hAh-beh-shah) get treated the way I was treated. As a foreigner (ፈረንጅ: feh-rIhnj), though, I have felt that sense of uncomfortableness numerous times. Typically, it doesn't get to that point. Yet, two days prior, as I was entering a bookshop with two friends, three guys outside were definitely waiting on us to exit so they could do something to us. It's really a pretty crazy feeling, a crazy experience.

Of the previous five times I had been to Ethiopia, I had never really had those types of interactions. I'm not sure if that boils down to me just being out more or sellers and others on the sidewalks getting more courageous and aggressive in their tactics. Whatever it is, when push came to shove in this case, it was time to give the pushy guy a well-earned shove.

Focal Words: Road (መንገድ: mEhn-gehd) | City (ከተማ: keh-tEh-mah) | Ethiopian (ሐበሻ: hAh-beh-shah) | (White) Foreigner (ፈረንጅ: feh-rIhnj)

Your Turn:

Vocabulary Review #1

Adoption (ጉዲፈቻ: gu-di-fAh-chah)
Alphabet (ፊደል: fEE-dehl)
America (አሜሪካ: ah-mEh-ree-kah)
Beautiful (ቆንጆ: qOhn-joh)
Bible (መጽሐፍ ቅዱስ: mEts'-haf qih-dUs)
Car (መኪና: meh-kEE-nah)
Children (ልጆች: lee-jOh-ch)
  *Child (ልጅ: lEEj)
City (ከተማ: keh-tEh-mah)
Coffee (ቡና: bU-nah)
Dad / Father (አባባ: ah-bAh-bah)
Daughter (ሴት ልጅ: sAyt lihj)
Ethiopia (ኢትዮጵያ: eet-yO-pee-ya)
Ethiopian (ሐበሻ: hAh-beh-shah)
Food (ምግብ: mAh-gihb)
Foreigner (White person) (ፈረንጅ: feh-rIhnj)
Friend (ጓደኛ: gwah-dEh-nyah)
Garbage Dump (ቆሻ: qOh-shay)
God (እግዚአብሔር: ig-zAhb-heyr)
Injera (እንጀራ: in-jEh-rah)
Man (ወንድ: wEhnd)
Money (ብር: bIrr)
Mother (እናት: Ih-naht)
No! (አይ: Aye)
Police (ፖሊስ: po-lEEs)
Rain (ዝናብ: zEh-nahb)
Rainy Season (ክረምት: keh-rImt)
  *Or: Winter
Road (መንገድ: mEhn-gehd)
Roundabout (አደባባይ: ah-deh-bAh-bay)
Tomorrow (ነገ: nEh-geh)
Water (ውሃ: wU-ha)
World (ዓለም: Ah-lehm)

What Is Your Future Plan?

Focal Words: I (እኔ: Ih-nee) | Amharic (አማርኛ: ah-mah-rEEn-yah) |
Teacher (አስተማሪ: ahs-teh-mAh-ree) | Doctor (ዶክተር: dOhk-tehr)

For the most part, I (እኔ: Ih-nee) enjoy being around kids. I suppose that at the moment of writing this, I am a little biased. My four children are seven, eight, nine, and ten years old and, frankly, kids of that age are the ones I enjoy the most. During my two months in Addis recently, I began to bond with many of the kids because I was seeing them just about every weekday.

One young girl, whom I shall refer to here as Meki, had been in the orphanage with her younger sister for nearly three years. Meki's smile was a mile wide and lit up an entire room. She was ten years old and had probably already seen and experienced more hardship in her life than I still have. Many days, Meki would act as my translator and, even though there were points when we couldn't quite understand each other, she consistently helped and impressed me.

It was only into the second or third visit, I believe, that Meki really began talking to me. She seemed to really like practicing her English. The first question I remember her asking me, one which left a marked impression on me simply because of how proper she sounded when she said it and how serious of a question it was for a girl her age to ask was, "What is your future plan?"

It was likely a question she herself had heard and been asked before but that didn't matter. After marveling at her inquiry for a moment, I responded by saying, "Well, I am a teacher." And she replied, with eyebrows raised to sky and a smile across her face, "Ah, in Amharic (አማርኛ: ah-mah-rEEn-yah), 'teacher' is 'astemari' (አስተማሪ: ahs-teh-mAh-ree)." I gave it a moment and then put the same question back to her. She responded saying that she wanted to be a doctor (ዶክተር: dOhk-tehr).

Her reason for wanting to be a doctor was because she spent years in an orphanage around sick babies. Sometimes those sick babies didn't make it and she wanted to help prevent that. Days later, my friend, John, who works as a physician's assistant, brought a stethoscope along and let her practice using it. The joy that exuded from her while she was listening to other kids' heartbeats and deep breaths was something I'll always remember. And I hope, from the deepest depths of my being, that one day she will be a doctor. She certainly has the potential and her country could certainly benefit from her serving in such a capacity. God forbid that she, like many others, are simply tallied up in the "wasted talent" category. Rather, I pray that her people will see the potential in her and realize what a great asset she can be to her people and those around her.

Focal Words: I (እኔ: Ih-nee) | Amharic (አማርኛ: ah-mah-rEEn-yah) | Teacher (አስተማሪ: ahs-teh-mAh-ree) | Doctor (ዶክተር: dOhk-tehr)

Your Turn:

Come On It!

Focal Words: And (እና: Ih-nah) | All Day (ሙሉ ቀን: mU-lu qehn) |
English (እንግሊዝኛ: ihng-lee-zIhn-yah) | Far (ሩቅ: rUq)

One of my favorite places in all of Ethiopia is the Highlands. More specifically, I love visiting the corner of earth known as Debre Libanos. In conjunction with the newly constructed Ethiopian Orthodox Church there, a number of myths and legends about fantastical religious individuals loom large. There is still a monk who lives in a cave and (እና: Ih-nah) there are still many long-held traditions at work.

In my previous travels to Debre Libanos, I had always hiked a steep and treacherous path along a rugged mountain face, up to flat pasturelands. This also allowed me to stand atop some of the amazing waterfalls that pour over the cliffs. This time, however, that wasn't possible. In fact, the priest who essentially guards the gate and charges foreigners to have a look around, expressly forbid me from trying to do so. He pointed out that a landslide had collapsed the trail and it was no longer passable.

Having driven nearly three hours to get there, which actually seemed like all day (ሙሉ ቀን: mU-lu qehn), I, along with two other friends, were a bit downcast about this. Yet, there were three little boys who, from the moment we pulled in and parked the car, were essentially glued to our sides. One young boy in particular, a twelve-year old named Reuben, lived in the area. His brother was there with him, too, and rather than being sent to a private or public school, their parents in Addis sent them way out here to Bible school. They had already spent years studying to be priests.

As a Bible scholar, I loved talking with Reuben about his studies. His English (እንግሊዝኛ: ihng-lee-zIhn-yah) was excellent but, unfortunately, he had been taught that Ge'ez, the first language of Ethiopia, which is now considered ancient and is only used in the church, was also the first language the Bible was written in. A bit perturbed by this fact, I sought a number of ways to try to inform

26

him that Hebrew and Greek (along with Aramaic, of course, which I didn't mention) were the first two languages the Bible was written in. Selling him on that was no easy task, however, for he had never really been faced with the challenge of having his studies or teachers questioned.

Eventually, talk about the Bible subsided and Reuben decided that he wanted to try to lead us through the forest to get closer to the waterfalls. A bit earlier, the priest had warned us to not go that far but Reuben and the other two kids insisted. And, again, since we had just driven three hours, we took him up on the offer. It was a hot day but, like many Ethiopians, Reuben donned a sweater and scarf but didn't seem to overheat at all.

About halfway through our journey to the base of the waterfalls (rather than the top), we stumbled upon the creek that resulted from the falls. There at a swimming hole there must have been a dozen young naked Ethiopian men bathing, swimming, and jumping off rocks into the water. One of those guys, Zeno, who was married and a university student, decided to join us. In fact, he took over as our makeshift tour guide.

Zeno took us back and forth across the creek, up and down sketchy rock slopes, and pointed out lots of things along the way. He was thin, fast, and also had great English. It seemed as though his favorite thing to say, something which I can still hear in my head as though he were sitting right here saying it, was "Come on it! Come on it, Mickey!" His inflection was catchy and the fact that he couldn't or wouldn't simply say "Come on!" fascinated me. It had to be "Come on it!" And then, of course, like many Ethiopians, he shortened my name to a nickname or term of endearment—it showed that he liked me.

I could say much more about that day but I don't really need to. While I am an avid waterfall enthusiast, and while there were some beautiful waterfalls I saw that day, it was Reuben and Zeno that made a lasting impression. They showed me a side of Debre Libanos that I hadn't necessarily seen before—a very personal side with a very local yet globalized twist. They were speaking *my* language after all. Thus, there, in the Highlands, far (ሩቅ: rUq) from home, I actually felt at home for a moment.

Focal Words: And (እና: Ih-nah) | All Day (ሙሉ ቀን: mU-lu qehn) | English (እንግሊዝኛ: ihng-lee-zIhn-yah) | Far (ሩቅ: rUq)

Your Turn:

Bribe at the Nile

Focal Words: River (ወንዝ: wEhnz) | Pen (እስክሪብቶ: is-krEEb-toh) | Head (ራስ: rAhs) | Upset Stomach (የሆድ መታወክ: ye-hOd meh-tAh-wehk)

About five-and-a-half hours northwest of Addis Ababa sits a rather non-descript town named Dejen. The ride there, unlike roads to many places, is paved and allows for rather *quick* travel. I emphasize the word "quick" there because there is not a car that travels on that road that goes slow. Every vehicle seems to move at top speed. And between the many potholes and moving human targets seemingly unaware that they are crossing a main highway, it takes some nerve to travel on it. Well, at least it has for me each of the six times I have.

But just below Dejen sits a river (ወንዝ: wEhnz) known as The Blue Nile (some refer to it as The Black Nile). It is a branch of "The" Nile that, much like the rugged terrain surrounding it, is beautiful but incredibly unforgiving. According to locals, it teems with wildlife such as snakes and crocodiles. Thus, when a local sixth-grader named Aschalew walked me down so I could dip my hands into the water, he was on high alert.

Little Aschalew didn't seem to concerned, however, about all of the baboons—animals often known for their violence—that surrounded the place. On the day I went, the water was rushing hard through the northern portion of the East African Rift Valley. The sun was also scorching, and at each side of the newly constructed bridge sat military guards armed and watching.

Even during Rainy Season, the heat at this rather low point was tough to bear, so, I and my two friends couldn't handle more than an hour there. On the hike from the river back up to our car, we grew exhausted. As we proceeded to leave, our young friend and impromptu guide, Aschalew, asked for a ride to the other side of the bridge; we gladly obliged. We dropped him off, said goodbye, and proceed to snake our way up the mountain we had earlier descended.

When we reached the top, however, we were flagged down by a traffic cop. My friend Sammy, a native Ethiopian who was driving for us, remarked that we were only being stopped because the police saw an opportunity—two white guys in the car. Indeed, that's exactly how it seemed. One of the officers, with the buttons on his uniform about to pop off due to his stomach pushing out, tried to make small talk with us at first while the other officer dealt with Sammy outside the car.

Quickly, however, the conversation turned. The officer who seemed kind and interested in us, pulled out a pen (እስክሪብቶ: is-krEEb-toh) and wrote on his hand. It was the number 2,500. Puzzled, I asked, "You want 2,500 birr from us?" (At that time, it was about the equivalent of $115.) He looked at me and shook his head (ራስ: rAhs) in the affirmative. Shocked, I tried to briefly switch the subject. I told him I had an upset stomach (የሆድ መታወክ: ye-hOd meh-tAh-wehk), due to the curvy roads, and that I needed to get back to Addis. He took a minute or two, listened into the conversation between Sammy and the other cop, and then leaned back through the driver-side window. He stuck his hand out again and, this time, he wrote 500 on it.

I looked at my friend, Chris, grabbed half of that from him, chipped in the other half, and before I handed it to him, I asked, "True?" In other words, I was asking if he was being honest. He shook his head yes and then I confirmed with the driver: "True?" He, too, confirmed. So, I handed him the money. They told Sammy that he would not be stopped anywhere else along the way back to Addis—guaranteed. So, Sammy got back in the car and we took off. Twenty miles down the road, however, we were flagged down again. This time we had a crowd of Oromo kids stand beside the car and watch.

The only difference was that this officer wasn't budging. And he wasn't looking for a bribe. He wasn't interested in bartering. He wrote a ticket for 2,500 birr because the rental car was, indeed, lacking a proper registration ticket. Needless to say, about 20 miles after that, the car overheated and we had to pull over, let it cool down, and replenish the coolant with leftover portions of bottled water. Thankfully, it worked and, a few hours later, we made it back to the city agreeing that, regardless of the trials, the journey together was worth it.

Focal Words: River (ወንዝ: wEhnz) | Pen (እስክሪብቶ: is-krEEb-toh) | Head (ራስ: rAhs) | Upset Stomach (የሆድ መታወክ: ye-hOd meh-tAh-wehk)

Your Turn:

Aster

Focal Words: School (ትምህርት: tihm-AIrt) | Banana (ሙዝ: mUz) | Book (መጽሐፍ: mEhts-haf)

Five years prior to writing this book, my wife and I decided to embark on the crazy journey of adoption again. We had adopted eight-and-a-half years earlier and, from start to finish, that was quite easy and only took a year-and-a-half. The second time around, however, things were not so simple. In fact, just about everything was difficult.

One of the most frustrating parts about the second attempt at adoption was the seeming incompetence of our agency or, more specifically, individuals working for our agency. They seemed to lack any desire to get work done in a timely fashion and, even after they promised frequent updates on our children, those updates never transpired. That's why, upon arriving in Ethiopia near the end of the fifth year to try to get work done myself, I was shocked to discover that my daughter had been attending a private school (ትምህርት: tihm-AIrt) for a year.

Moreover, I learned that she was being sponsored by another family. Here I was, her father, and all I could think that that should have been my job. But since the agency never did check-ins and since they sucked at communicating, why would they have known these things? In fact, they didn't know where my son attended a different school, or where he was going week in and week out either.

Nevertheless, it was a delight to know that every day of the week she was getting out of the orphanage and receiving clean water, food, a safe atmosphere, and an education. And it was a very special moment for me to attend her school on Parents Day and meet her teacher, see her grades, and get to know the place a bit better.

That day was a rainy day and I had my driver pick up the mother of two other girls who also lived at the same orphanage as my daughter. The mother, Aster, was separated from her daughters for a few years by sheer economics. She had a sidewalk banana

(ሙዝ: mUz) gig going, where she made very little from day to day. After the second daughter was born, her husband left her. She had not been to the school prior but, on this day, I sat with her, my daughter, her daughters, and numerous other kids in the school library. As I read book (መጽሐፍ: mEhts-haf) after book, she sat and listened and held her kids. She seemed happy.

She was also able to see her oldest daughter do a science experiment presentation in front of a group of people. And she witnessed her youngest daughter win an award or two for her academic excellence. So, right alongside watching my daughter and experiencing this moment with her, I kept an eye on Aster, too. It was a joy to help her make it there, a joy to watch family be reunited.

I had only meet Aster two weeks before at the orphanage. The language barrier hindered us from saying much more than the standard greetings, but her presence there intrigued me. So, I sought to stay in touch with her. Interestingly, during week four of my stay in Addis, I was actually able to witness this mother regain custody of her two girls and bring them home. Thankfully, the girls were able to continue attending school, despite living on the other side of the city, and, at the same time, once again be with the woman they loved so much. I hope they can stay together!

Focal Words: School (ትምህርት: tihm-AIrt) | Banana (ሙዝ: mUz) | Book (መጽሐፍ: mEhts-haf)

Your Turn:

Play Guitar

Focal Words: You (አንተ: Ahn-teh) | Give! (ስጠኝ: sih-t'Ehn) | Black (ጥቁር: t'Ih-qur) | Lion (አንበሳ: ahn-bEh-sah) | Hospital (ሆስፒታል: hos-pEE-tahl)

Having been to Ethiopia a little more than a handful of times, I've had my fair share of people approach me and ask me for money. As a foreigner, especially a white foreigner, I feel magnetic at times. A friend of mine, a native Ethiopian, tells me that as soon as people see my white skin, their first thought is "Get money from him!" He also says that, at some point, especially for the kids, their parents must have told them, "When you see a white person, quickly ask for money."

Based on my experiences, what he says seems on point. This is no less true in the countryside than in the city. It is an everyday thing to have people approach me in that manner. With folks like this, there are no hellos, no how are yous, and no other conversation starter. Instead, one hears "You! (አንተ: Ahn-teh) three times in a row or "Money give (ስጠኝ: sih-t'Ehn)!" It's incredibly off-putting but perhaps that's just my Western sensitivities, I don't know. I have constantly attempted to try to see things from their perspective but that doesn't seem to make things any easier to understand.

There was one occasion, however, where one-by-one, locals started approaching me for another reason: I was playing guitar on the sidewalk. It was late at night, about 9pm and I was standing on the sidewalk with my friend, Chris, waiting for my taxi. We had carried the guitar out of the SIM missionary compound, which is located near the infamous Black (ጥቁር: t'Ih-qur) Lion (አንበሳ: ahn-bEh-sah) Hospital (ሆስፒታል: hos-pEE-tahl).

As I waited on my taxi, I strummed the acoustic guitar and sang. I played and sang some classic rock like Skynard's *Sweet Home Alabama*, as well as some hip hop, like a modified and cleaned-up version of Nelly's *Ride Wit Me*. Quite quickly, the locals out on that Friday night circled and watched. When I stopped for a moment, many clapped and extended their hands for a handshake. Then they introduced themselves and asked where I was from, also inquiring as to how I was and what I thought about Ethiopia. I was reminded then that music can, indeed, make the world a better place because it has the ability to bring together the unlikeliest of people and unite them in a most unusual way. "Oh sweet home!"

Focal Words: You (አንተ: Ahn-teh) | Give! (ስጠኝ: sih-t'Ehn) | Black (ጥቁር: t'Ih-qur) | Lion (አንበሳ: ahn-bEh-sah) | Hospital (ሆስፒታል: hos-pEE-tahl)

Your Turn:

I See You in My Dreams

Focal Words: New (አዲስ: Ah-dees) | Letter (ደብዳቤ: dehb-dAh-bay) | Sister (እህት: ih-hEht) | I Love You! (እወድሻለው: ih-weh-dih-shAh-low)

The art of letter-writing is something of a lost art in America. Honestly, I can't recall the last time someone wrote a letter for me by hand. Truth be told, the letter is one of the most intimate and ancient forms of communication. Even the New Testament contains letters from the Apostle Paul to a number of congregations he attempted to keep open lines of communication with.

I suppose that with the advent of email and texting, letter-writing just isn't as easy and convenient. Recently, I wrote two letters for my daughter while she was away for the first time at church camp for five days where, each day, she received a new (አዲስ: Ah-dees) letter (ደብዳቤ: dehb-dAh-bay). My wife also wrote two, but my other daughter, still in an orphanage in Ethiopia at the time, also wrote one.

I asked her if she would write one for her sister (እህት: ih-hEht) and she didn't hesitate. She asked for a paper and pen and went off for about fifteen minutes or so. When she returned, she handed it to me along with a nice little envelope she had created, too. She was a little shy about me having a peek at the letter but, since it was in Amharic, I figured I had better give it a look and ask for some translation help.

The letter was very short and pretty much centered like a poem. It started out with my daughter's name—the one at camp. Then, the next four lines read: 1) I love you. (እወድሻለው: ih-weh-dih-shAh-low) 2) Sometimes 3) in my dreams while sleeping 4) I see you. And twice more it repeated "I love you," the second of which replaced the word "love" with a heart symbol.

When I read that, my jaw dropped and I could barely hold it together. There I was, standing in the middle of a playground at an orphanage in Ethiopia, all-out stunned. Of all the things she could

36

have said, much less mature and more kid-like things, she said this. Unbelievable! So, I returned to the hotel, took a photo of the letter, and sent it off to my wife back in the States. She then emailed it to camp, which proceeded to print and deliver it. It was as close to hand-written as we were able to get given the time and distance gap.

After camp, my wife asked my daughter who received the letter, "What did you think of that?" And without even missing a beat, she replied, "Oh yeah, I see her in my dreams a lot, too." And when my wife told me that, once again, a jolt hit me. I, the father of these two sisters, one in Ethiopia and one in America, sat in awe. I thought to myself, "My daughters, who have never met, are seeing each other in their dreams!"

While my default stance is to refrain from attributing things to God right out of the gate, whether good or bad, something about that just felt like God. I don't know if I'll ever be able to put a finger on the mysteriousness of it all, but it is incredible to me. It is overwhelmingly incredible to me. And in some deep and profound way, it captures the essence of adoption for me. And the beauty of writing letters.

Focal Words: New (አዲስ: Ah-dees) | Letter (ደብዳቤ: dehb-dAh-bay) | Sister (እህት: ih-hEht) | I Love You! (እወድሻለው: ih-weh-dih-shAh-low)

Your Turn:

19 Strangers & 2 Chickens

Focal Words: North (ሰሜን: sEh-mayn) | Yesterday (ትናንት: tEh-nahnt) | Chicken (ዶሮ: dOh-roh)

When I was a teenager, there was a television show that came out titled "Faces of Death." Because of its gory and gruesome nature, some of the other guys really acted as if they were into it—they thought there was a certain "cool factor" to watching it. I, however, had no interest. It's just not my thing; it never has been and never will be. The appropriate hashtag here might be #SorryNotSorry.

But…on the day before I penned this entry, I must admit, I was thinking about death. More particularly, I was thinking about a very specific way I would not want to die: in an Ethiopian mini-bus. I was thinking this because I had just been north (ሰሜን: sEh-mayn) of Addis and, on the way there, saw many crashed, crushed, and flipped over mini-buses. Riding on that long stretch of road known as Highway 3, well, let's just say that it's not at all for the faint of heart. Not at all!

While much of Ethiopian culture seems laid back and not in a hurry, that's not the culture of Highway 3. There, everyone seems to be in a hurry. High-speed passes on blind curves, 2-ton trucks swerving across lanes to dodge pot holes, and the plethora and animals and people walking out in front of speeding cars, that's the norm. I've never seen anything like it anywhere else in the world. For me, I don't really know where the nerve to keep riding on that road comes from—maybe I just naively get into the car and go.

Yesterday (ትናንት: tEh-nahnt), however, I didn't want to die. I was riding in a private taxi, a tiny, silver, 4-seat, stick-shift, Toyota Vitz—a popular car in Ethiopia. And I cannot even begin to count how many mini-buses flew past us in an amazingly reckless fashion. One had even hit a pedestrian head-on!

Later that night, when I returned to my hotel, a friend shared a video with me. It was a minute-and-a-half long phone scene of cell-phone captured footage showing one of those same mini-buses turned sideways in a strong rushing creek. Even more, it was sitting right at the top of a waterfall and looked as if it was about to go over. People were climbing out the side windows of the bus, one at a time, and catching a rope that someone on the bank was throwing to them. The individuals, standing on the half-submerged mini-bus, would grab the rope and effectively jump-swing over the water to the bank. Amazingly, everyone made it out alive.

That's a way I would not want to die. So, I told myself I would avoid those mini-buses as long as I could. But as fate would have it, I ended up riding in several across the city the very next day. Granted, it is a bit safer to ride in them in the city, but not by much. For instance, the small bus/van I was in had nine seats, including the front two. Yet, I counted and there were 19 people aboard and…two chickens. That's right, there were people sitting in the floor, standing bent over, sitting on laps, and, in the midst of it all, one live chicken (ዶሮ: dOh-roh) with its leg tied to the other, both sitting on the floor clucking.

That kind of thing would never fly in America but, in Ethiopia, it's the norm. In fact, when I was telling a friend about this, she was a bit surprised saying, "Really?! There should've been room for two or three more people; they were wasting space." I could only laugh at that. Well, I laughed for a minute and then I winced a bit because the thought came to mind again that I didn't want to die that way—surrounded by 19 strangers and 2 chickens.

Focal Words: North (ሰሜን: sEh-mayn) | Yesterday (ተናንት: tEh-nahnt) | Chicken (ዶሮ: dOh-roh)

Your Turn:

Pick Just One Word

Focal Words: Government (መንግሥት: mEhn-gihst) | Word (ቃል: qAhl) | Wife (ሚስት: mEEst)

As an American, there are many things I love and enjoy about my country. I have, for instance, a deep love for the beautiful scenery spread across the United States. And I enjoy the freedom I have to move about as I please. But there are also things that I despise or even hate about America. I despise the racism and brutality and rush to arms so often put on display by various government (መንግሥት: mEhn-gihst) institutions. And I hate how the culture has become obsessed with sexuality, especially many of its more perverse forms, and preys on children and teenagers in that regard. So, I have something of a love-hate relationship with my country.

Although I am not a citizen of Ethiopia, I have been here enough times and stayed here long enough to get a good feel for things. And similar to my own country, I have a kind of love-hate relationship with this place. I love so many of the beautiful, kind, and good-hearted people. I enjoy the Highlands and the richness of the land. But I loathe all the littering and disrespect for the land, especially in the city. And I struggle with some of the government institutions that seemingly take forever to get a few pieces of paperwork processed. Just as well, my heart breaks at the level of destitution and suffering I see in many slums and even just on the street corner.

Well, recently, a friend and I were walking down the sidewalk and he asked, "So, if you could use one word (ቃል: qAhl) to describe Addis, what would it be?" I thought about that for quite a long time before I could answer. I struggled and struggled to find just one word. So, I did the next best thing I could, I mashed a few words together. I remembered my wife (ሚስት: mEEst) using the word "brutiful" at some point in the past and, so, I got hung up on that. But it wasn't enough, therefore, I added to it: brutifeudal.

40

Brutifeudal is a mash-up of three words: brutal, beautiful, and feudal. The notion of brutal came to mind because, for many, life is just that. It is incredibly difficult, difficult beyond measure for some. But there is, as I said moments ago, lots of beauty in this place—the people and the land. Yet, there is also a hint of feudalism. That term is usually employed when talking about the Medieval Era, the Middle Ages.

A feudal society is one where the power brokers sit at the top and wield authority and control of the people. They do things like seize land that isn't theirs and then either use it for their own or parcel it out. And many times they have no real concern about what goes on with the commoners, they are simply to fend for themselves. As a result, society tends to take on an anything-goes mentality. Respect for self and neighbor is often lost in the attempt to merely preserve oneself. I do see elements of that in Ethiopia all around.

So, "brutifeudal" was my word on Sunday. But as I was driving through a rain storm on Monday morning, another term, perhaps more apt, came to mind. It arose while sitting at one of a handful of stoplights in the center of the city. Out my window I saw one of the main streets flooding and, in the background, lots of unfinished buildings soaring into the air. There were also beggars of every age standing and sitting in the rain seeking a handout.

The word that came to mind this time was "unfrastructure." For me, unfrastructure has to do with the race to build and build and build while not realizing that the underlying infrastructure to do so is not present. This is seen in flooding roads, poor plumbing, flawed electricity, semi-functional technology, substandard living, substandard health practices and medical services, unsanitary lifestyles, and the inability to care for millions who are sick, displaced, and dying.

Another term that comes to mind, one that stems from conversation with a friend, is "post-apocalyptic." This is the idea that there *used to be* a place with a solid infrastructure but, in the wake of a disaster, what remains only partially works—it works just well enough to get by with some comfortability. Essentially, it's a place of unfrastructure. Now, lest I seem too negative here, I want to reiterate that I was asked to only choose one word. And, for the life of me, I can't escape the fact, especially coming from a first-world setting, that the daily hardships that folks face here stick out to me more than just about anything.

But to be fair, I have been asking native Ethiopians lately what they like about their country. Some of the things I've heard are "the beautiful, joyful people," "the traditions," "the culture," "the closeness of family," and "the food." Every one of those responders, however, also expressed frustration with the government—even if they supported it in one way or another. Ultimately, however, I'm not finished answering my friend's question; this is something I'll continue to ponder for a while, perhaps a lifetime. But for now, I'll leave it at that.

Focal Words: Government (መንግሥት: mEhn-gihst) | Word (ቃል: qAhl) | Wife (ሚስት: mEEst)

Your Turn:

Vocabulary Review #2

All Day (ሙሉ ቀን: mU-lu qehn)
Amharic (አማርኛ: ah-mah-rEEn-yah)
And (እና: Ih-nah)
Banana (ሙዝ: mUz)
Black (ጥቁር: t'Ih-qur)
Book (መጽሐፍ: mEhts-haf)
Chicken (ዶሮ: dOh-roh)
Doctor (ዶክተር: dOhk-tehr)
   *Doctor (ሐኪም: hAh-keem)
English (እንግሊዝኛ: ihng-lee-zIhn-yah)
Far (ሩቅ: rUq)
Give! (ስጠኝ: sih-t'Ehn)
Government (መንግሥት: mEhn-gihst)
Head (ራስ: rAhs)
Hospital (ሆስፒታል: hos-pEE-tahl)
I (እኔ: Ih-nee)
I Love You! (እወድሻለው: ih-weh-dih-shAh-low)
Letter (ደብዳቤ: dehb-dAh-bay)
Lion (አንበሳ: ahn-bEh-sah)
New (አዲስ: Ah-dees)
North (ሰሜን: sEh-mayn)
Pen (እስክሪብቶ: is-krEEb-toh)
River (ወንዝ: wEhnz)
School (ትምህርት: tihm-AIrt)
Sister (እህት: ih-hEht)
Teacher (አስተማሪ: ahs-teh-mAh-ree)
Upset Stomach (የሆድ መታወክ: ye-hOd meh-tAh-wehk)
Wife (ሚስት: mEEst)
Word (ቃል: qAhl)
Yesterday (ተናንት: tEh-nahnt)
You (አንተ: Ahn-teh) (for a male)
   *You (አንቺ: Ahn-chee) (for a female)

An Interlude - Vocabulary Review #3:
36 New Words You Already Know

Thus far you have encountered and, perhaps, internalized 64 Amharic words. At this point, I want to offer an interlude of sorts, that is, a brief and intervening section that will help boost your confidence a bit more. I hope to do that by pointing out to you that, by virtue of knowing English, there are already at least 36 Amharic words you already know—although, some do have just a slightly different pronunciation. I should say, too, that some of these words, while used in or are closely connected with English, may derive from other languages like French, Greek, Hebrew, or Italian.

By the way, if you're quick on your feet, you've likely already done the math and realized that this brings your total word count to 100. So, rejoice because after you finish this interlude, you'll have a handle on your first 100 Amharic words. As usual, the English word is provided first, the Amharic script/spelling second, and a transliteration of the Amharic third. (Note: *The words "Doctor, Hospital, and Police," could also fall into this list but, since you've already learned them, they are not included here. Also, this of course, is not an exhaustive list but rather a partial and selective one.*)

Academy (አካዳሚ: ah-kAh-dah-mee)
Airplane (አውሮፕላን: ahw-rOhp-lahn)
  *Sometimes spelled differently (አይሮፕላን: ayih-rOph-lahn)
Battery (ባትሪ: bAht-ree) – this can also mean "flashlight" in Amharic
Bravo! (ብራዎ: brAh-woh)
Cake (ኬክ: kAyk)
Candy (ከረሜላ: kah-rah-mAy-lah)
Christian (ክርስቲያን: krIhs-tee-yahn)
Ciao (ቻው: chAhw)
Cigar (ሲጋራ: see-gAh-rah) – or cigarette
Coat (ኮት: kOht)

Coca Cola (ኮካ ኮላ: kOh-kah kOh-lah)
Computer (ኮምፒውተር: kohm-pEEw-tehr)
Diploma (ዲፕሎማ: deep-lOh-mah)
Film (ፊልም: fEElm)
Hello (አሎ: Ah-low) – especially when answering phone
Jacket (ጃኬት: jAh-kiht)
Jesus Christ (ኢየሱስ ክርስቶስ: ee-yay-sUs krEEs-tohs)
Mango (ማንጎ: mAhn-goh)
Music (ሙዚቃ: mU-zee-qah)
Muslim (ሙስሊም: mUs-leem)
Office (ቢሮ: bEE-roh) – think "bureau"
Papaya (ፓፓያ: pah-pAh-yah)
Pepsi (ፐፕሲ: pEhp-see)
Photo (ፎቶ: fOh-toh)
Pizza (ፒዛ: pEE-zah)
Politics (ፖለቲካ: poh-lEh-tee-kah)
Post (ፖስታ: pOhs-tah) – as in "mail"
Printer (ፕሪንተር: prEEn-tehr) – refers to a machine, not a person
Salon (ሳሎን: sah-lOhn)
Science (ሳይንስ: sAh-yihns)
Sofa (ሶፋ: sOh-fah)
Soft Tissue (ሶፍት: sOhft)
Sport (ስፖርት: spOhrt)
Sugar (ስኳር: sIhw-kahr)
Taxi (ታክሲ: tAhk-see)
Zipper (ዚፕ: zEEp)

A 13-Step Guide to Printing 2 Pages in Ethiopia

Focal Words: Day (ቀን: qEhn) | Morning (ጠዋት: t'Eh-waht) | Minute (ደቂቃ: dEh-qee-qah)

Dear reader, if you had a nickel for every time I said the words "difficult" or "challenging" during my most recent trip to Ethiopia, you would likely be rich. I uttered those words many times throughout the day (ቀን: qEhn), usually with an accompanying sigh and/or headshake. No, nothing came easy or was accomplished without enduring some sort of grueling process.

For instance, as I was heading out the door of the hotel one morning (ጠዋት: t'Eh-waht), I urgently needed the front desk to print a two-page document for me. But this seemingly simple event turned into an incredibly elaborate undertaking. It took 13 steps, across a span of about 50 minutes (ደቂቃ: dEh-qee-qah), to print 2 pages. What follows are those steps. I offer them so that if you ever find yourself here and in a similar situation, you'll know just what to expect and do.

Step 1: Go to the hotel lobby and visit the reception desk and ask them to print a couple of pages for you. If your files are on a USB stick like mine were, be prepared for the computer not to recognize the stick.

Step 2: Since the computer downstairs will not recognize the USB device, head upstairs to the manager's office on the third floor. But be prepared for the door key (either electronic and traditional) not to work.

Step 3: Wait for the manager to attempt to find another key (either electronic and traditional). But don't expect it to work either.

Step 4: Watch the manager use an old-school technique to pick the lock to the office. Don't worry about informing him that he's just demonstrated how to pick the lock to his office. It won't matter, seriously, it just won't.

Step 5: When you enter the office and see two computers, choose the computer to the right. At this point, go ahead and have a seat while the manager fires up the computer. Don't expect, however, that he'll have the username or password.

Step 6: Wait a bit while the manager calls to reception and asks if they remember the login information. It would, however, be best not to get your hopes up.

Step 7: At this point, you'll probably consider going ahead and trying the computer on the left side of the room. Go ahead. When you get it to boot up and recognize your thumb drive, go ahead and open the document and click the printer icon. Now you're printing!

Step 8: Joyfully go and retrieve the paper from the printer. But…

Step 9: Don't be surprised when the printer is essentially out of ink, so much so that the ink on the page isn't really legible. You might squint at it, look at it from different angles, and try to justify it. But you'll soon come to the realization that it's just not going to work.

Step 10: So, head back down to reception and try the computer there once more. I mean, if the one upstairs recognized your USB stick, maybe this one will, too. Maybe the first try was just a fluke. Be on guard, however, because even though the computer will recognize it this time, ultimately, it's going to corrupt it and make it impossible to access and/or find your files.

Step 11: While mumbling a few choice words under your breath, hop a taxi and go to the first local print shop you see. You'll notice that it's a print shop by looking at the banner above the front door. When you walk in and see all the computers there, get ready for a surprise. When you ask if you can print a file from your USB stick, they'll tell you they're out of ink. (Okay, by this point maybe it's not all that surprising.)

Step 12: Get back in the taxi and drive around until you hit another printer shop. Once again, as you enter, notice all the computers. And just as confidently as you ask them if they'll print a file from your USB stick, be confidently ready to walk out because they, too, are out of ink.

Step 13: Give it one more try. Third time's a charm, right?! Hit up another print shop and, after waiting in line for 10 minutes (that's actually a good sign at this point!) ask them if they can print a file from your USB stick. When they say "Yes." rejoice. You have undertaken and overcome a major feat. Congratulations, you now know how to print a two-page document in Ethiopia.

Focal Words: Day (ቀን: qEhn) | Morning (ጥዋት: t'Eh-waht) | Minute (ደቂቃ: dEh-qee-qah)

Your Turn:

T.I.A.

Focal Words: Month (ወር: wEhr) | Year (ዓመት: Ah-meht) | Sun (ጸሐይ: ts'eh-hAh-yih)

"13 Months of Sunshine." That's a tagline you'll likely either see or hear at some point if you travel around Addis Ababa. To the Westerner it seems crazy. It seems impossible. It seems illogical. It might even seem like a gimmick. There must be some catch, right?

The truth is: Ethiopia has its own calendar and, yes, it actually does have 13 Months. It's actually quite logical. 12 of the months contain 30 days. The last month (ወር: wEhr), Pagumen, actually only has 5 or 6 days depending on whether it's a leap year (ዓመት: Ah-meht). It's kind of interesting and pretty cool. The more you know!

Another interesting fact is that, during Rainy Season, which is more like winter for Ethiopians, that sunshine often vanishes rather quickly. It takes no time for dark clouds to roll in and vanquish the rays of the sun (ጸሐይ: ts'eh-hAh-yih). Then, in an instant, you might be met with a forceful rain, hail, and/or a cold front. And guess what? After all that, the sun will often pop right back into view and dry things up. It's pretty wild!

But during those storms, one thing you're sure to encounter is a lack of power. It is very common for the electricity to go out during a storm. While most places are equipped with generators, many are not. I sat for 45 minutes in a federal government building, for instance, in the dark. During that time workers were in a meeting and it didn't seem to faze them. They pulled out their cell phones and used the light from them to see one another.

And it's at that point, in a situation like that, that you'll hear a common phrase: T.I.A. That's simply an acronym for "This Is Africa." The implied sentiment here is, of course, that it's a developing country and, therefore, these types of things should be expected. Even though I don't really like the statement and what it implies, I suppose that in my experiences with Ethiopia, there seems to be quite a bit of truth to it. But it also worries me that it is part of the societal mindset because it promotes a deterministic or fatalistic outlook that stands little chance of cultivating anything positive.

Or maybe its just the locals truly being able to laugh in the midst of struggle and hardship. Either way, I feel a bit odd when I, as an outsider, say it. For me, it's like the old I-can-make-fun-of-my-family-but-you-better-not mentality. For now, however, I'll continue to wrestle with such things.

Focal Words: Month (ወር: wEhr) | Year (ዓመት: Ah-meht) | Sun (ጸሐይ: ts'eh-hAh-yih)

Your Turn:

Alemsehaye

Focal Words: Language (ቋንቋ: kwAhn-kwah) | Eye (ዐይን: Ah-yihn) | Mouth (አፍ: Ahf)

Sometimes there just are not words. Sometimes that's because the situation is so emotion-laden and raw that, in that moment, speech simply does not get the job done—it seems empty. And sometimes there are not words for other reasons, very practical ones, like a language (ቋንቋ: kwAhn-kwah) barrier. Despite what most people seem to think, when two people speak different languages, turning up the volume and saying it repeatedly gets nobody nowhere fast.

But sometimes, in spite of the language barrier, one desperately needs communication to take place. If there is no translator, what does one do? Sometimes gestures work. Sometimes using objects works. But recently, I encountered a woman with whom I needed to talk named Alemsehaye. Even though she couldn't speak a lick of English and my Amharic was broken at best, we found a way: eye (ዐይን: Ah-yihn) contact.

In a way, it was a bit of a surreal experience. I'm not sure I've ever had someone look me in the eyes the way she did. Alemsehaye was an older woman, probably in her late fifties or early sixties, and was a caretaker at the orphanage where my son lived in Addis. I hadn't really seen her before but she came squarely into view on one specific day because she knew I needed help and she knew I was trying to do a good thing.

I was attempting to help a teenage boy get his documents in order so he could get to school in the United States. A few friends had invested some time and effort into this, too, but were hitting dead ends. Well, the dead end I hit was the orphanage director, a woman named Tigist. Stated quite frankly, Tigist was lazy. She showed up at the orphanage to basically eat lunch, drink coffee, and have a lunchtime chat with some of the caretakers. Not once did I see her playing with kids, holding kids, or investing in the kids.

In fact, when I showed up one day and my son was gone, she said that he was at school. When I asked the name of the school she didn't know it. When I asked where it was at, she didn't know. When I asked how that could be, she had no response. That got me heated!

I was also heated on the day I was attempting to help this teenager because she, as the director, was refusing to help. All we needed was the boy's birth certificate. But he didn't have one. And to add to that, both of his parents were deceased so he couldn't rely on them to get him one. And so, Tigist said, "Impossible!" That, actually, is a very common phrase in Ethiopia. Impossible! (Ugh! I got so sick and tired of hearing that. But, just in case you're eager to hear more, I'll devote an entire story to that saying later.)

After a few minutes of me trying to argue with Tigist with limited ability, Alemsehaye walked up. She stood and observed, watching with great patience. The irony is that the name Tigist means 'patience' but it was Alemsehaye who embodied it. Anyway, as she watched the broken back-and-forth between me and Tigist, I noticed her staring intently at me. Actually, her stares were more like soul penetrating gazes.

Although she didn't speak English, I knew should could understand me. Her eyes told me so. It may well have been the closest I've ever been to an experience like that of Pentecost in the early chapter of the biblical Book of Acts. It was as if I was speaking my language but she was hearing hers—I don't know. All I know is that her eyes told me, "Don't worry, I've got you!" And once I realized that, I just shut up and she took over. It was incredible.

After she addressed Tigist for the first time, Tigist's response was the same: "Impossible!" But Alemsehaye shook her head in defiance and uttered two English words: "Yes, possible!" She looked at me with a smile on her face when she said that. For a moment, I felt like I had won some sort of championship prize. For me, that was a linguistic experience *par excellence*. But the crazy thing is, it was a linguistic experience done mostly with the eyes rather than the mouth (አፍ: Ahf). I'll never forget that unique moment.

Focal Words: Language (ቋንቋ: kwAhn-kwah) | Eye (ዐይን: Ah-yihn) |
Mouth (አፍ: Ahf)

Your Turn:

Lily's Nail

Focal Words: Restroom (ሽንት ቤት: shIhn-tih-bayt) | Traditional Ethiopian House (ጎጆ ቤት: gOh-joh bayt) | Kid (ሕጻን: hEh-ts'ahn) | Foot (እግር: Ih-gihr)

On the city outskirts of Addis there is an amusement park for young children. It's non Six Flags but neither does it attempt to be. Heck, it's not really even up to par when it comes to a local county fair. But in some sense, *maybe* it's better than nothing. (Notice that I emphasized "maybe" in that last sentence on purpose.)

The name of the theme park is Lily. It has a carousel-like ride but with cars instead of horses that blares a mix of English and Amharic kids tunes. There's also a spinning chain swing ride and several kiddie cars that move up and down as if floating on waves. They play music, too, and since they sit right across circling motorcycles, the songs clash. It just sounds like a lot of noise.

There's a two-person trampoline missing springs and with holes in the net—it resembles the shape of the trampolines I saw while growing up in the trailer park. There's also a regular swing that two people can swing side-by-side on and it sits next to a bouncy house. There's a restroom (ሽንት ቤት: shIhn-tih-bayt) under a small and nearly caved-in hut or Traditional Ethiopian House (ጎጆ ቤት: gOh-joh bayt).

Yes, there's all of that, but what stuck out to me most was the ferris wheel. For the first 45 minutes of being there, I actually thought that it was broke down. Turns out, I was wrong. You see, a friend and I had brought a busload of nearly 60 kids to Lily and, once they had filed through all the rides, the only thing left was the wheel. It looked like it had survived a couple wars and when the worker came to fire it up, he sent it around once and then proceeded to clean the left-over vomit from previous riders out of one of the buckets. Umm…that was gross!

As he did that, another worker was lining each kid (ሕጻን: hEh-ts'ahn) up and placing them into a group of 3 or 4. Once the ride was ready, children started filing up the short set of five steps to the platform that allowed them to take a seat. But I noticed something after a handful of kids had already made their way up: the wooden bottom step was flipped upside down, which meant one of the nails was sticking straight up. In the short amount of time from when I noticed that to when I could get over to it, I saw two kids step on that nail. One had flip flops on. That nail drove right through her shoe and into her foot (እግር: Ih-gihr). When I saw that, I had a nasty cringe. It didn't really seem to affect her; instead, she just looked down at it and kept moving.

When I got to the step, I ripped off the bottom step and threw it near a wall where nobody was standing. In my head I was thinking, "If the workers didn't even notice that the bottom step was a safety hazard, how in the world are these kids going to survive this ride?!" But those youths were either incredibly naïve or had some sort of bravery that I no longer embody. In fact, I stepped way off to the side just in case that wheel came loose and started rolling down the hill and into the busy street below.

Eventually, all the kids got their ride and, to my disbelief, they all survived. And to top it all off, they all got an ice cream cone on the way out the gate. Those kids were in the zone. It was the first time they had been on anything resembling a vacation in three years. My friend, Chris, who was leading this trip, had taken then out three years prior, too, to a few different places. While Lily was a surprising sight, I think we might consider an alternative next time. I guess that's just the concerned parent in me.

Focal Words: Restroom (ሽንት ቤት: shIhn-tih-bayt) | Traditional Ethiopian House (ጎጆ ቤት: gOh-joh bayt) | Kid (ሕፃን: hEh-ts'ahn) | Foot (እግር: Ih-gihr)

Your Turn:

An American Man

Focal Words: White (ነጭ: nEhch') | Family (ቤተሰብ: bay-teh-sEhb) | Mud (ጭቃ: chIh'qah)

The first time I came to Ethiopia, it rocked my world. Not having had any prior experience in third-world or developing countries, I'm not sure anything could have prepared me for it either. Seeing things here gave me a new perspective. For example, in America I grew up poor by most standards. I was what some people would affectionately dub "trailer trash" or "white (ነጭ: nEhch') trash."

The thing is, we always had a car, always had a roof (although, we did move very often), always had food, always had clothes, always had a clean school to go to, and *almost* always had running water and electricity (they only got shut off a few times). But still, in the United States, my living situation would be viewed as poor. Some might even refer to it as poverty.

But in Ethiopia one doesn't see poverty. No, in Ethiopia, one sees destitution. In my view, there's a very big difference, even chasmic perhaps. Here many people in the city still have dirt floors, a 10x10 living space made out of mud (ጭቃ: chIh'qah) and sheet metal (or aluminum), and beg for a living. Many have no water to eat or food to drink and no job to earn either. It's this kind of thing that is a major contributor to the world orphan crisis—sheer economics prevents the family (ቤተሰብ: bay-teh-sEhb) from staying together.

And, so, there's a lot of desperate people here. And while some aren't afraid to let you know it, some do try to be a bit more tactful in conveying the gravity of their situations. Recently, I met a woman named Hiwot whom I liked quite a bit and whom was probably somewhere between the two examples just mentioned.

Hiwot was raised, from the cradle to young adulthood, in government orphanages. When it was time for her to go, she was actually offered a job as a caretaker at the last orphanage she had spent her teen years in. At one point, she had a daughter but her daughter's daddy walked out on both of them when the little girl was born. It is a perfect example of how the cycle of hardship and destitution is perpetuated. What she has going for her, at least, is that she has employment.

But within an hour of meeting Hiwot, she handed me a picture of herself. It was a headshot about 2 inches by 2 inches, kind of like you'd see on a passport or visa. Moreover, it looked like it was from 7 or 8 years earlier. When she handed me her picture, she said, "Please, give this to an American man. Please, tell him to marry me, to come find me and marry me. It will be easy for you to find me a man in America, yes?" I tried to explain that such a feat would not be nearly as easy as she imagined but, given the language barrier, I'm not sure that was conveyed clearly or registered clearly.

So as not to cause any hard feelings, I went ahead and took the headshot. In fact, it's sitting on the desk next to me as I write this. I spent a few moments just prior to writing thinking about whether or not there was a person I could actually give this to. Unfortunately, nobody came to mind. And while her giving me this tiny photo and requesting this favor might be off-putting to some, it doesn't really bother me. Why? Because I can't blame someone who, in living in a state of desperation day in and day out, tries in an honest and upfront way to make the most of an opportunity when they see one. Here, opportunity just doesn't come knocking very often. In fact, for some, it never does.

Focal Words: White (ነጭ: nEhch') | Family (ቤተሰብ: bay-teh-sEhb) | Mud (ጭቃ: chIh'qah)

Your Turn:

The Stupidest Thing I've Heard All Day

Focal Words: Window (መስኮት: mEhs-koht) | Weekend (የሳምንት መጨረሻ: yeh-sAh-mihnt meh-chEh-reh-shah) | Again (እንደገና: ihn-dEh-geh-nah)

How people make it into positions of influence and power in Ethiopia is not really a mystery. Much of it simply comes down to connections. And many of those connections, at least within the government, are tribe-based. For instance, Tigre people make up only 7% of the population in all of Ethiopia but they hold nearly all of the political power. So, if you are from the Tigre people and want a position of influence, as long as you have some connections, you should have no trouble being slotted into such a role in due time.

That is not to say, of course, that only those with a Tigre background are hired into the government. That's not at all the case. Rather, my point is that sometimes it's not education or merit that lands someone a job of significance, but rather tribal background. So, when education and merit are chucked out the window (መስኮት: mEhs-koht) or have the brakes put on them, that becomes problematic. It creates a system of top-down injustice and has the potential to generate a cascade of problems.

Recently, I met an orphanage director who, based on his logic, probably shouldn't have been in the position he was. This was a guy functioning as the director who, on one specific day, was the winner of the "that's the stupidest thing I've heard all day" award. That award was created and given by me, of course.

Circumstances forced me into talking with this man, whom I shall refer to here as Willy. I had to speak with him because, after waiting out a very long weekend (የሳምንት መጨረሻ: yeh-sAh-mihnt meh-chEh-reh-shah) to see my daughter (the government orphanages don't allow visits on the weekend), when I arrived where I had been seeing her for weeks, she was moved. So, I had to find the new place she was moved to. While I was on great terms with the director of the previous orphanage, I now had to wade into unfamiliar territory

58

and attempt to get on this guy's good side, too.

After speaking with him for a few minutes, he told me I actually wasn't allowed to visit. That, in and of itself, was infuriating. He told me I needed to get permission to be there. So, I had to call the previous director and she told me I had to get a letter from the government to get access. Since I knew what I had to do, I did it.

Once I took him the letter, he let me start visiting during the day. But, a day in, I learned that he was preventing all the girls who had been moved, my daughter included, from attending the private school they were sponsored. So, I tried to talk with him again (እንደገና: ihn-dEh-geh-nah) and tried to convince him to reconsider. He just wasn't having it. Once again, he told me I'd need to get a letter of approval from the same government office. When I asked him why he wouldn't let them attend school, he remarked, "How can I let them go to a private school when all the other girls have to go to a government school?"

In talking with my friend Chris about this and sharing my frustration, he broke things down in a rather clear way. I want to share that with you. So, I give an overview/summary of what he said.

Premise 1 (Willy's premise): If all of the children are not enrolled in private school, then none will attend the private school.
Premise 2: Not all of the children are enrolled in the private school.
Conclusion: Therefore, none of the children will attend the private school.

This, he says, is a *modus ponens* deductive syllogism. Now, that's a bit wordy so let me explain what it means. Simply put, it's a type of logic or argumentation that assumes that if Premise 1 is valid, then it means that Premise 2 must be valid. And if both premises are valid, then the conclusion must also be valid. The problem is: just because a form of argumentation is valid, that doesn't mean that it is necessarily true. For instance:

Premise 1: If I eat pizza every Monday, then I gain two pounds.
Premise 2: I eat pizza every Monday.
Conclusion: Therefore, I gain two pounds (every Monday).

One can easily see that while this is a valid form of arguing, it isn't necessarily true in what it concludes. Why? Because I could eat only one piece of pizza on a certain Monday because I just wasn't all that hungry. Or I could eat a low-fat pizza one week but not the next. Or I could eat so much that I actually more gained weight. Thus, different variables can result in different outcomes.

So, back to my friend, Chris. His retort was, "This man needs to justify his reasons for Premise 1, which is impossible." It's impossible to justify because the government, whom he works for, "sanctions private schools and the children have already been enrolled and attending. Therefore, he has no authority to deny them their rights." So, the real problem is that this man, an orphanage director, is actually not appreciating the rights of children.

When I returned to the government office to request a letter to be written for all of the children whom this orphanage director was holding back, his boss was also frustrated. And unknowingly echoing Chris's sentiment, she remarked, "He has no right to do that. He has no right to withhold them from education." An hour later, I had a letter from her. It was signed, officially stamped, and I delivered it to him in person on behalf of the kids and the school. The next day, they were back in school. And they have been ever since for the letter demanded that Willy allow them to return. That was the best thing I had heard all day.

Focal Words: Window (መስኮት: mEhs-koht) | Weekend (የሳምንት መጨረሻ: yeh-sAh-mihnt meh-chEh-reh-shah) | Again (እንደገና: ihn-dEh-geh-nah)

Your Turn:

Gezahegne's Flip

Focal Words: Countryside (ባላገር: bah-lAh-gehr) | Truck (ካሚዮን: kAh-mee-yohn) | Ball (ኳስ: kwAhs)

Imagine standing before a firing squad but without a blindfold and no cuffs. And imagine being told that, on the count of three, they'll start firing at you but you're actually allowed to move to try to get out of the way. In short, you would literally be dodging bullets.

Personally, I don't know anyone who would do such a thing voluntarily. Most of us realize that life's simply too precious to do such a thing. For some reason, however, here in Ethiopia I see people doing this kind of thing basically every day. In fact, remove the tiny piece of steel, the bullet, from the equation, and replace it with a piece of steel that weighs a few thousand pounds or even a ton and that's precisely what you see in Addis.

Driving (or riding) through the city, or even the countryside (ባላገር: bah-lAh-gehr) for that matter, is like witnessing people dodge speeding bullets that weigh thousands of pounds. This happens all day every day. That is not an exaggeration whatsoever. In fact, within the city I have noticed a couple of billboards warning both pedestrians and drivers about this.

I actually saw a children's book, one version in Amharic and another in English, with a drawing of a dead child lying in the road that had just been hit by a truck (ካሚዮን: kAh-mee-yohn). He was wearing a yellow polo shirt and blue jeans and right next to his side was a ball (ኳስ: kwAhs), which, presumably, he went to retrieve. The caption read: "I don't play in the middle of the road. Playing on roads is dangerous. It also makes it difficult for cars to move."

While I'm not sure how many Ethiopian children will see this book, the message it sends is on point. In fact, this message may be even more apropos for the parents reading to their children. Especially parents like Gezahegne, a man who ran out in front of the taxi I was riding in and ending up flipping over the hood and rolling off on to the road. Gezahegne was a big guy both in height and width. Thus, he left a pretty good-sized dent in the hood of the car. I am happy to report, however, that he didn't die.

He was grimacing in pain, as one might expect, immediately after the hit. He was holding his lower back and yelling loudly. Since this happened downtown, within 30 seconds people had swarmed our car and surrounded us. I was legitimately wondering if a mob attack was going to ensue. But nothing of the sort happened. Word has it that when a car gets encircled like that, it's so the driver doesn't take off.

Well, our driver didn't take off; rather, he stuck around. And instead of calling the police or an ambulance, he and the victim talked it out face to face. The deal they shook on was that the driver would help pay the initial hospital visit for Gezahegne to get checked out. Since my driver had to get me somewhere and couldn't go with him to the hospital right away, he simply gave him his license as a goodwill gesture. Turns out, Gezahegne never even went to the hospital, didn't ask for any money (although, we did think he was trying to do so at first), and returned the license the next day. I think after our initial shock we were all surprised by the final outcome.

Focal Words: Countryside (በላገር: bah-lAh-gehr) | Truck (ካሚዮን: kAh-mee-yohn) | Ball (ኳስ: kwAhs)

Your Turn:

A Shoestring Budget

Focal Words: Pants (ሱሪ: sU-ree) | Backpack (የጉዞ ቦርሳ: yEh-gu-zoh bOhr-sah) | Shoestring (የጫማ ማስሪያ: yeh-chAh-mah mah-sEh-ree-yah) | Next Day (በማግስቱ: beh-mAh-gihs-tu)

Ethiopians are nothing if not resourceful. You can drive through the city and see sculptures made out of plastic water bottles. You can see walls with glass shards cemented in at the top instead of barbed wire. And one of my personal favorites was seeing a few children quickly tear up a cardboard box as the rain started to roll in. They each took a piece of the cardboard, grabbed a branch, and jammed it through the middle finally treating it as if were an umbrella. Very creative and resourceful!

I think a bit of that rubbed off on me when, one day at the orphanage, my daughter's pants (ሱሪ: sU-ree) were too big for her and sliding off her. She was walking around holding her hot pink pants by the belt loops so they'd stay up. At first, I tried folding the top of the pants over but that didn't really work; they were still too big. Then I remembered that I had a shoestring (የጫማ ማስሪያ: yeh-chAh-mah mah-sEh-ree-yah) in my backpack (የጉዞ ቦርሳ: yEh-gu-zoh bOhr-sah). I unzipped the pack and got it out.

I then proceeded to weave the shoestring through her belt loops. When I made it all the way around, I simply tied a bow and, voila, it worked. The case of the constantly-falling-down-pants was now solved. And, not surprisingly, when I came back the next day she had the same pants on and she had managed to tie the string herself. And the same was true of the next day (በማግስቱ: beh-mAh-gihs-tu). That little trick worked well. Sometimes that's what you have to do in Africa—operate on a shoestring budget.

Focal Words: Pants (ሱሪ: sU-ree) | Backpack (የጉዞ ቦርሳ: yEh-gu-zoh bOhr-sah) | Shoestring (የጫማ ማስሪያ: yeh-chAh-mah mah-sEh-ree-yah) | Next Day (በማግስቱ: beh-mAh-gihs-tu)

Your Turn:

Vocabulary Review #4

Again (እንደገና: ihn-dEh-geh-nah)
Backpack (የጉዞ ቦርሳ: yEh-gu-zoh bOhr-sah)
Ball (ኳስ: kwAhs)
Countryside (ባላገር: bah-lAh-gehr)
Day (ቀን: qEhn)
Eye (ዐይን: Ah-yihn)
Family (ቤተሰብ: bay-teh-sEhb)
Foot (እግር: Ih-gihr)
Kid (ሕፃን: hEh-ts'ahn)
Language (ቋንቋ: kwAhn-kwah)
Minutes (ደቂቃ: dEh-qee-qah)
Month (ወር: wEhr)
Morning (ጠዋት: t'Eh-waht)
Mouth (አፍ: Ahf)
Mud (ጭቃ: chIh'qah)
Next Day (በማግስቱ: beh-mAh-gihs-tu)
Pants (ሱሪ: sU-ree)
Restroom (ሽንት ቤት: shIhn-tih-bayt)
Shoestring (የጫማ ማሰሪያ: yeh-chAh-mah mah-sEh-ree-yah)
Sun (ፀሐይ: ts'eh-hAh-yih)
Traditional Ethiopian House (ጎጆ ቤት: gOh-joh bayt)
Truck (ካሚዮን: kAh-mee-yohn)
Weekend (የሳምንት መጨረሻ: yeh-sAh-mihnt meh-chEh-reh-shah)
White (ነጭ: nEhch')
Window (መስኮት: mEhs-koht)
Year (ዓመት: Ah-meht)

Tis'net's Hug & Kiss

Focal Words: Saturday (ቅዳሜ: qih-dAh-may) | Park (መናፈሻ: meh-nAh-feh-shah) | Smart (ነቢዝ: gOh-behz)

Coordinating a day trip where one has to rent a bus large enough to hold 60 kids is no easy feat. Finding fun places to take them only adds to that challenge. On a Rainy Season Saturday (ቅዳሜ: qih-dAh-may) that managed to keep the skies clear and bright for us, we made such a trip go off without a hitch. It was a great day.

For me, the start of it was particularly special. We had four scheduled stops on the agenda that day, the first being a small town outside of Addis. Here there was an old, defunct Ethiopian Airlines passenger plane situated so that it was part of the kids park (መናፈሻ: meh-nAh-feh-shah) it sat right next to. It was quite neat and, well, since the park could make money off of letting kids run through it, it was a pretty smart (ነቢዝ: gOh-behz) business deal, too.

And for many of those kids, living in the toughest of situations near the Addis city dump, it might actually be the only time they ever step foot on a plane. So, after feeding them, we had the kids line up single file in front of the stairs that allowed entry up to the plane door. There was a gentleman dressed in an Ethiopian Airlines flight attendant uniform who granted a few of the kids access at a time.

While they were taking their places in line, I sat on a tiny cement wall just behind the line. Behind me some of the kids were swinging and playing on merry-go-round-like rides. I was looking around just trying to soak the moment in when a little girl, about 5 years old, appeared out of nowhere and nuzzled her head into the crook of my neck. I didn't know this little girl but that was no problem.

She leaned into me for a moment and then with her big brown eyes looked into mine. I don't know what gave her the inkling to do it but then she stretched her little self up and planted a tiny kiss on my left cheek. And then she hugged me and smiled. After that she simply jumped into line and proceeded to board the plane. Perhaps she was just so happy and thankful that she needed a way to express it, I don't know. What I do know is that it made my day and made me thankful, too.

Focal Words: Saturday (ቅዳሜ: qih-dAh-may) | Park (መናፈሻ: meh-nAh-feh-shah) | Smart (ጎበዝ: gOh-behz)

Your Turn:

Coming Back

Focal Words: Time (ጊዜ: gEE-zay) | Hour (ሰዓት: seh-Aht) | Week (ሳምንት: sah-mIhnt) | Bedroom (መኝታ ቤት: mehn-yEh-tah bayt)

Nostalgia is a powerful thing. The way that a smell, sound, sight, feeling, or any other trigger can take us back to a time (ጊዜ: gEE-zay) or place or circumstance is something I find phenomenal about our innate humanness. When people sit around and trade "war stories" or talk shop or share about the good ol' days, it often seems driven by an underlying attempt to touch the nerve of nostalgia.

While in Ethiopia, my daughter, who had spent close to two years in a government-run orphanage, was moved. There was no heads-up about this; it just happened. There was a bit of a panic moment for me there, where I was wondering if she had gone to a specific place, a worse place, that others had warned me about. Indeed, she had!

There was one day, however, when I was able to take her back, just for an hour (ሰዓት: seh-Aht) or two to the place she had lived for two years. It hadn't even been a week (ሳምንት: sah-mIhnt) but given the way she walked around and looked at things, one would have thought that a) she had never been there before, or b) she was an incredibly inquisitive child in super deep thought.

Since many other kids had also been moved, the place that was formerly filled with little ones running free range was now rather quiet. She didn't know what to think of it. She did see the younger children she knew there and embraced them in a big sister sort of way. Given that it was sparse and quiet I was anticipating that we could have a little time to ourselves for once. But that didn't happen.

Instead, she wanted to revisit the bedroom (መኝታ ቤት: mehn-yEh-tah bayt) where her old bunkbed was, see the babies she was missing, and play with one of her friends—a daughter of one of the caretakers who spent her days at the orphanage playing with the kids. So, I didn't force the issue; rather, I let her do what she wanted.

It was almost like a chance to heal from the grieving she had experienced from the move.

I had heard that she and many of the other little girls were so upset and crying hard when they arrived. Like me, the girls received no forewarning and simply were not prepared for it. In an instant, they were just uprooted at the whim of the government. For a kid with little to nothing, stability is invaluable. And when that rug is pulled out from under your feet, the world itself might as well have been turned upside down.

Thus, it was a nostalgic kind of day. It was what she needed and although I, in a fierce dad-loving way, wanted her to hang out with me, I could sense that she just needed this time. I wanted to let the nostalgia offer some balm to her soul if it could. I think it did. I remain in awe, however, about how fond this little girl was of a place that I and many others only seem to see the negative about. That day I realized that my daughter's joy can run deep. She can make this world a better place. And at times like this, she can humble me and teach me and make me a better man.

Focal Words: Time (ጊዜ: gEE-zay) | Hour (ሰዓት: seh-Aht) | Week (ሳምንት: sah-mIhnt) | Bedroom (መኝታ ቤት: mehn-yEh-tah bayt)

Your Turn:

Plaid Shoes, Flannel Shirt

Focal Words: Shoes (ጫማ: ch'Ah-mah) | Boy (ወንድ ልጅ: wEhnd lihj) | Shirt (ሸሚዝ: sheh-mEEz)

All over Addis Ababa are young children known as "shoeshine boys." Based on the caricature, it's not difficult to guess what they do—shine shoes (ጫማ: ch'Ah-mah) for a living. Most of these boys are between about 7 and 16 years old. They sit on the sidewalk all day with a dirty bucket of water by their side, a couple of rags if they're fortunate to have that many, and a bit of soap. They work hard, often get screwed over and mistreated by clients, and are viewed pretty low on the social ladder.

In all the times I've been here, I've never been able to sit myself down in front of one of those boys. It just doesn't seem right for some reason, even though I'd likely be helping them by giving them a little money. In fact, in what little I might give, many of them have adult bosses watching who will take a cut of each bit made from cleaning someone's shoes.

I remember looking out the window of the guest house I was staying in several years ago each morning. Without fail, there would be the same group of 3 boys there, waiting for a shine. So, I started taking breakfast out to them because I knew they were hungry. Well, after a few days of doing that, I happened to get back to the guest house and look out the window when, lo and behold, an adult was slapping one of the boys and taking that breakfast. It! Was! Infuriating!

I knew I couldn't march back out and address the situation because it would cause a big scene and that, along with any kind of trouble, was the last thing I wanted. Yet, I felt guilty all the same for not going. On this recent trip, however, I ended up using a shoeshine boy to clean a pair of newly purchased shoes. Well, I actually didn't hire him, the shop owner did. The new shoes, by virtue of not sitting far from a road that had thousands of cars pass by in traffic every day, were dirty.

70

So, after the purchase, the shopkeeper motioned for the shoeshine boy (ወንድ ልጅ: wEhnd lihj) to come over. He was a young boy, probably 9 years old, with a red and black flannel shirt (ሸሚዝ: sheh-mEEz) on. He had black jeans with holes in them and red knock-offs of Converse's Chuck Taylor All-Stars. The tongues on his high tops were huge and flopping over his laces. And there he was, kneeling down on the ground cleaning a pair of plaid slip-on shoes that I had just purchased for my daughter, who was also 9 years old.

And I couldn't help but think, "Right now my daughter is in school about 2 miles up the road. In fact, she is in a private school. Why isn't he in school, too?" And then, "When was the last time someone bought him a gift, something like shoes?" And, "What will his life be in comparison to hers?" I couldn't help that these thoughts were flooding my mind but they did.

I realized then and there that when I'm here, for some reason, every little thing seems to be magnified. It's like I'm hyper-aware and that my senses are hyper-sensitive. Every detail seems to stick out in a way that, at home in the States, doesn't really seem to happen. I don't know if it's because these are not my routine experiences at home or if it's because things are just so different here or what. I don't exactly know. But that's just how it is. Thus, I don't even know how to react when a young boy sits on the ground before me to clean the new shoes I just bought my daughter. I'm not sure I could ever get used to seeing it. It's tough.

Focal Words: Shoes (ጫማ: ch'Ah-mah) | Boy (ወንድ ልጅ: wEhnd lihj) | Shirt (ሸሚዝ: sheh-mEEz)

Your Turn:

Not Possible!

Focal Words: Question (ጥያቄ: t'ih-yah-qAy) | People (ሕዝብ: hIh-zihb) | Many (ብዙ: bIh-zu)

Lately, I've been attempting to analyze a common phrase I've heard countless times while in Ethiopia—"Not possible!" I've heard the phrase enough times from enough different people to begin to think that it is a mentality that is built into the society fabric of this country. It's that thought that has led me to ponder where this might have started or at least where some of it may have taken root. At this point, I can simply venture some guesses because I have not had the requisite time, space, or resources to try to plumb the depths of this question (ጥያቄ: t'ih-yah-qAy).

But one of my thoughts is that, perhaps it stems from several things. One might be, for example, the long history of not having arts in the educational system, especially the system run by the government. Thus, free thought, creativity, questioning, and spontaneity were never woven into the daily lives of generations of people (ሕዝብ: hIh-zihb). In fact, those things may well have been purposefully suppressed.

Another thought is that the Chinese government, with its large-looming presence here, has brought with it an essentially Communistic flavor. Like China, the Ethiopian government has the ability to control land, has the ability to open or close down the internet at will, and keeps a tight lid on free speech—especially when it is critical of the government. All of this makes many (ብዙ: bIh-zu) things truly seem impossible.

But it trickles down to the smallest of things, too. For instance, when I asked at a restaurant if I could have my pineapple smoothie made with bottled water instead of tap water, the response I received was, "It's not possible." At another restaurant there were several types of pasta on the menu, one with marinara sauce only and another with olives in it and no marinara sauce. So, my friend asked if he could simply order the marinara pasta and have the olives put on it—he was willing to pay extra. Without a blink, the waiter responded, "Sorry, it's not possible."

Another friend told me of a story where a colleague went into a local shop seeking something like duct tape. The owner of the shop told him that they were currently out of it. There was, however, a roll sitting in the store window on display. When he asked the shop owner if he could just buy that, yep, you guessed, "No sir, it is not possible." These few instances are but snapshots of the microcosm that, in my experience, reflects the macrocosm.

To be sure, I have encountered this frustrating statement again and again. Most of the time I'm left speechless for a moment. I stand there thinking about how basic problem-solving skills seem to be totally absent and why in the world that is. Sure, I have my guesses but the reality is, I've probably not even scratched the surface of the matter. But, after all, maybe it's not possible.

Focal Words: Question (ጥያቄ: t'ih-yah-qAy) | People (ሕዝብ: hIh-zihb) | Many (ብዙ: bIh-zu)

Your Turn:

Genet

Focal Words: Gate (መዝጊያ: mEhz-gee-yah) | Or (ወይስ: wEhys) | She (እሷ: Ihs-wah)

There are few greater things to witness in this life than a child leaving an orphanage forever. With my own children, I have been able to see that three times now. Witnessing that child walk out the gate (መዝጊያ: mEhz-gee-yah) for the last time has so much symbolism. At a minimum, it represents freedom, hope, opportunity, new life, and family.

As I write this, however, Ethiopia is looking to shut down international adoptions. The claim is that the country is going to focus on in-country adoptions, that they are ready to do so. But talk to just about any local and they will tell you that nothing could be farther from the truth. While I have met Ethiopians who are adopting, not a single one of them lives in Ethiopia—they all live in the United States or (ወይስ: wEhys) elsewhere.

I wish this weren't the case but it is. And apart from being heartbreaking, it is frustrating. It is like seeing those orphanage gates closed and locked from the inside—nobody's getting out. In spite of my frustrations with this entire issue, when I step back I am reminded that there are many folks serving the government who are more than cogs in the machinery of the political wheel. Indeed, there are some—perhaps many, but I don't know—who are working hard and striving to make a difference. There are some who take seriously the fact that their job is to help and advocate for children.

One such person, a friend named Genet, has amazed me time and time again. She (እሷ: Ihs-wah) has repeatedly gone above and beyond. She has stopped mid-day to write letters for me, she has walked in at 9am to find me already waiting in her office only to greet me with a smile, she has taken my phone calls, she has helped my friends, and most of all she has always put children in need first. There aren't enough words to express how grateful I am for her!

It is because of people like Genet that children are able to have a chance. My hope and prayer is that she will continue to advocate for them in the future as she does now, a future where the fate of adoption seems to hang in the balance. And I pray, too, that her drive, spirit, and mindset will rub off on those around her. For, I simply shudder at the thought of those orphanage gates never opening again. May that never be the case!

Focal Words: Gate (መዝጊያ: mEhz-gee-yah) | Or (ወይስ: wEhys) | She (እሷ: Ihs-wah)

Your Turn:

Playing Games

Focal Words: Paperwork (ወረቀት: weh-reh-qEht) | Signature (ፊርማ: fIh-rih-mah) | Job (ሥራ: she-rah) | Rock (ድንጋይ: dIhn-gah-yeh) | Leg (እግር: Ih-gihr)

When you're in the adoption process and you travel to Ethiopia, for the most part, your time spent in country is "all business." There's little time to have fun or play. Chasing down paperwork (ወረቀት: weh-reh-qEht) and trying to get a new signature (ፊርማ: fIh-rih-mah) each day is one's job (ሥራ: she-rah). Although driving through the city sometimes feels like a game of real-life Frogger or Russian Roulette, at other times you simply make up games.

During my recent trip, since we were constantly being called out for being white foreigners, we decided to join the fun and come up with a game of our own: Feringe Finder. The game could be played at least two ways (as of now): 1) You get some points for finding a white foreigner, or 2) You hedge your bets before play ensues about how many foreigners you'll see. In the first, obviously, the person with the most points wins. In the second, the person who gets closest to their guessed number wins. For those traveling to Ethiopia, I commend this fun little game. Maybe even put your own spin on it.

A friend of mine here, a native Ethiopian, was taught by an American friend of my how to play "Punch Buggy." He kind of liked the game but he decided to turn it into a more Ethiopian version. His thinking was, since there are so many men urinating just about everywhere in the city at any given moment, why not make it about that. This is now affectionately known as "Pisser Punch." You already know how to play: instead of punching someone whenever you spot a Volkswagen Bug, but his idea was to punch them when you see a guy relieving himself in public.

A fun game I created is based around the many business signs all over Addis. This game does not require keeping points but simply being on the lookout as a group. The idea is to see how quickly you can spot a funny sign due to it being misspelled. I can promise you, it won't take long at all. Some of my favorites are "Toyota Spear Parts," "Earobics," and the many "Wel Come" signs spread across the city.

At my son's orphanage, the kids put their own spin on soccer, too. In their version it's everyone for themselves. If, at any point, someone kicks the ball between your legs and it goes through, everyone playing has an endless amount of punches or kicks that they can land on you until you touch a certain designated wall. This game is fun...if you're the one getting to punch and kick and not trying to dodge the punches and kicks. I learned quickly that these kids will show no mercy at all. There's frequent crying involved in this one, so, you have to have some nerve to play.

One game my daughter introduced me to was an Ethiopian version of hopscotch. I still don't quite understand it clearly but it has several rounds and involves throwing a rock (ድንጋይ: dIhn-gah-yeh) and landing it in specific squares. You then hop, sometimes on one leg (እግር: Ih-gihr) and sometimes on two, to retrieve the rock. You can't touch lines or you're out, you can't throw into the wrong square or you're out, and you have to do quite a bit of jumping that, if you land erroneously, puts you out, too. I realize I didn't explain this hopscotch game with the most clarity but, again, I don't know all the details. But be forewarned: if you show up at an orphanage with older kids, you better be ready to play.

And if you're ever headed to such a place, to get in the spirit or mood, try a few of the games mentioned above on the ride over. It'll pass the time a bit more quickly and might even relieve some stress. In my opinion, those are good things.

Focal Words: Paperwork (ወረቀት: weh-reh-qEht) | Signature (ፊርማ: fIh-rih-mah) | Job (ሥራ: she-rah) | Rock (ድንጋይ: dIhn-gah-yeh) | Leg (እግር: Ih-gihr)

Your Turn:

I Wanna Hold Your Hand

Focal Words: Guard (ዘበኛ: zeh-bEh-nyah) | Name (ስም: sIhm) | Happy (ደስተኛ: dEhs-teh-nyah) | Game (ጨዋታ: ch'Eh-wah-tah)

In Ethiopia it's not an uncommon sight to see persons of the same sex expressing their friendship through holding hands. Unlike the connotation that would be expressed in the United States, in Ethiopia there is nothing at all sexual about this; it has nothing whatsoever to do with same-sex attraction. In fact, homosexual activity is forbidden by law here and, by and large, everyone views it as a sin, an abomination before God.

Recently, when visiting the orphanage where my daughter was staying, one guard (ዘበኛ: zeh-bEh-nyah) there was eager to hold my hand. Concerning him and the other guards, I had spent weeks befriending them, getting to know them, learning their names, and building rapport. It is often incredibly difficult to visit a government-run orphanage and, so, having these folks on your side is a good thing and can often go a long way. It was also a form of social capital that could pay dividends for my daughter when I wasn't present.

The guard's name (ስም: sIhm) was Yosef. He was probably in his late forties or mid-fifties. His sense of humor was pretty good and he was always very happy (ደስተኛ: dEhs-teh-nyah) to see me. He loved trying to practice English with me and, in the process, being an on-the-spot Amharic teacher for me. On one certain day, however, he just grabbed my hand and held it. Prior to this, nobody had done such a thing.

Admittedly, I felt a little uncomfortable. Never in my life can I recall holding one man's hand. I have held others' hands during sporting events or prayer, but never individually like this. But, as I said, I wanted to keep a good relationship so I obliged. He just wanted to stand and chat for a while. Others came up and talked, too, and didn't think anything of it…it was completely normal.

Eventually, I wanted to go spend some time with my

daughter. (My routine was to spend the first fifteen or so minutes at the orphanage engaging the guards and others.) I don't know if she sensed that because she was around but, soon enough, she called me over to play a game (ጨዋታ: ch'Eh-wah-tah) with her. And that was the end of my hand-holding session. It was a unique experience for me to say the least. To riff off that old Roman saying, my thinking was, "When in Ethiopia, do as the Ethiopians do." So, I did.

Focal Words: Guard (ዘበኛ: zeh-bEh-nyah) | Name (ስም: sIhm) | Happy (ደስተኛ: dEhs-teh-nyah) | Game (ጨዋታ: ch'Eh-wah-tah)

Your Turn:

Lean On Me

Focal Words: Second (ሁለተኛ: hu-lEh-teh-nyah) | There (እዚያ: Ihz-yah) | Song (ዘፈን: zEh-fehn)

Every time I've visited Ethiopia, I've been quite shocked to see some of the specific things imported from the West. Without a doubt, American-style clothing is one thing that has been exported here. Fashion is picked up through television, the internet, movies, and the like. Music is also another item that has taken on widespread cultural consumption. It is not at all uncommon to hear American songs on the radio mixed in with Ethiopian songs.

One morning when visiting my daughter's elementary school, I heard several very familiar songs. In their morning warm-up, in order to start the day off right and build confidence, they sing "If You're Happy and You Know It" and also "Lean On Me." I can't explain how floored I was to hear them sing the second (ሁለተኛ: hu-lEh-teh-nyah) one. It completely caught me off-guard, but in a good way. I was thoroughly impressed.

About a dozen of the kids at that school were housed at the same orphanage as my daughter. So, when visiting and pulling my phone out to play some songs one day, the first thing I heard was a request for "Lean On Me." I didn't realize I had it on my phone but, after a bit of scrolling through the playlist, there (እዚያ: Ihz-yah) it was. So, I pushed the play button and it was like a choir came out of the woodworks.

All the kids who went to school together gathered around and started singing. Out of the three entire verses and the chorus, I believe they were able to go two verses deep knowing all the words to the song (ዘፈን: zEh-fehn). It was neat to not only witness this but to also be able to sing along with them. Indeed, there we were, standing in front of an old dilapidated swing set in Ethiopia belting out a 1970s Bill Withers tune together. It was a sight, and sound, of beauty. I'll always remember that. It's something that I'm sure will help me carry on!

Focal Words: Second (ሁለተኛ: hu-lEh-teh-nyah) | There (እዚያ: Ihz-yah) | Song (ዘፈን: zEh-fehn)

Your Turn:

Vocabulary Review #5

Bedroom (መኝታ ቤት: mehn-yEh-tah bayt)

Boy (ወንድ ልጅ: wEhnd lihj)

Game (ጨዋታ: ch'Eh-wah-tah)

Gate (መዝጊያ: mEhz-gee-yah)

Guard (ዘበኛ: zeh-bEh-nyah)

Happy (ደስተኛ: dEhs-teh-nyah)

Hour (ሰዓት: seh-Aht)

Job (ሥራ: she-rah)

Leg (እግር: Ih-gihr)

Many (ብዙ: bIh-zu)

Name (ስም: sIhm)

Or (ወይስ: wEhys)

Paperwork (ወረቀት: weh-reh-qEht)

Park (መናፈሻ: meh-nAh-feh-shah)

People (ሕዝብ: hIh-zihb)

Question (ጥያቄ: t'ih-yah-qAy)

Rock (ድንጋይ: dIhn-gah-yeh)

Saturday (ቅዳሜ: qih-dAh-may)

Second (ሁለተኛ: hu-lEh-teh-nyah)

She (እሷ: Ihs-wah)

Shirt (ሸሚዝ: sheh-mEEz)

Shoes (ጫማ: ch'Ah-mah)

Signature (ፊርማ: fIh-rih-mah)

Smart (ጎበዝ: gOh-behz)

Song (ዘፈን: zEh-fehn)

There (እዚያ: Ihz-yah)

Time (ጊዜ: gEE-zay)

Week (ሳምንት: sah-mIhnt)

Vocabulary Review #6:
25 More New Words You Already Know

Note: For some of these terms that are alternative words. Those listed here, however, are in common use and, in some instances, have replaced older and/or alternative terms (not listed here).

Acid (አሲድ: Ah-seed)
Amen (አሜን: Ah-mayn)
Arcade (አርኬድ: Ahr-kayd)
Bank (ባንክ: bAhnk)
Beer (ቢራ: bEE-rah)
Café (ካፌ: kAh-fay)
Cinema (ሲኒማ: sEE-nee-mah)
Clinic (ክሊኒክ: klEE-neek)
College (ኮሌጅ: kOh-lehj)
Condom (ኮንዶም: kOhn-dohm)
Embassy (ኤምባሲ: Aym-bah-see)
Fanta (ፋንታ: fAhn-tah)
Hallelujah (ሃሌሉያ: hah-lay-lU-yah)
Hotel (ሆቴል: hOh-tehl)
Kilogram (ኪሎ: kEE-loh)
Million (ሚሊዮን: mEE-lee-yohn)
Minister (ሚኒስትር: mIh-nih-stirh)
Mobile (Cell) Phone (ሞባይል: mOh-bah-yihl)
President (ፕሬዚዳንት: prAy-zee-dahnt)
Radio (ራዲዮ: rAh-dee-yoh)
Sprite (ስፐራይት: SprAh-yiht)
Stapler (ስቴፕለር: stAyp-lehr)
Television (ቴሌቪዥን: tAy-lay-vee-zhihn)
The (ዚ: zEE)
Visa (ቪዛ: vEE-zah)

Chasing Butterflies, Catching Crickets

Focal Words: In (በ: bEh) | Building (ሕንጻ: hIhn-ts'ah) | Wall (ግድግዳ: gEhd-geh-dah) | Face (ፊት: fEEt)

It seems that no matter where you go in (በ: bEh) the world, some things are just inherently the same. One of those, in children especially, is the desire to play. I've been to numerous places across the globe and that seems to be a universal, a constant. It's a great and I would even argue, necessary thing. Moreover, it's fun to watch and even better to participate in.

While sitting on the stoop of an old building (ሕንጻ: hIhn-ts'ah) in the orphanage compound one day, I sat with my back against the wall (ግድግዳ: gEhd-geh-dah) and watched three little boys play. Their names were Dagem, Lewid, and Kalahab (or something like that...that's the best I could gather from what they told me). Their game of choice was not soccer, for the grass in the yard was much too high to kick a ball, and they weren't interested in swinging or playing on the monkey bars either.

Instead, they were hunting insects. They were chasing butterflies, grasshoppers, crickets, and lizards. The boys were, quite interestingly, working as a team. They would spot one of the aforementioned insects and then narrow it in using a sort of triangulating pattern. I was having lots of fun just watching them.

My daughter was giggling as she watched, too, and actually ended up taking an uncountable number of videos and pictures of them. Every time one of the boys caught something, they would proudly bolt over to the stoop and show it off. They loved dangling the insects in front of my face (ፊት: fEEt). Surprisingly, they had no interest in smashing the insects or killing them or torturing them like many other kids might. For them, the thrill was in the chase, in the hunt.

If they couldn't nab something with their bare hands, a feat which they were quite adept at, they would often try using their coats. For instance, at one point a butterfly flew past them and

Dagem, holding his coat in a stretched-out fashion, proceeded to hurl it toward the butterfly like a net. It worked.

At the end of their hunting escapades, the trio came over and my daughter was excited to show them the photos and footage she had gathered. They sat there next to me fascinated by seeing themselves on camera. They laughed and laughed and laughed. For that reason, this tiny portion of one of my days just stuck out to me. It put me in a good mood. It reminded me of the power and importance of play. It reminded me that these kids are no different than kids anywhere else in the world, but that they were simply dealt a tougher hand than many. There they were in that moment, however, "playing" that hand well and with much joy.

Focal Words: In (በ: bEh) | Building (ሕንጻ: hIhn-ts'ah) | Wall (ግድግዳ: gEhd-geh-dah) | Face (ፊት: fEEt)

Your Turn:

Linoy

Focal Words: Crazy (እብድ: Ihbd) | Page (ገጽ: gEhts') | No problem!
(ችግር የለም: chIh-gehr yEh-lehm) | Thank you! (አመሰግናለሁ: ah-meh-seh-gih-nAh-leh-hu)

Sometimes life is crazy (እብድ: Ihbd); indeed, it can be
insanely crazy. Sometimes there's just no way to prepare for the
things you might see or hear or the people you'll meet. I write this
just a few hours after meeting a woman named Linoy in the United
States Embassy in Ethiopia. My encounter with her was, in my
estimation, kind of crazy—unbelievable, really.

On the day I met Linoy, I was standing at window #14 in the
Embassy. I was there to get a couple of pieces of paperwork
notarized and, unbeknownst to me, for every page (ገጽ: gEhts') that
needed notarized, I needed to have $50 on hand. So, I needed $100. I
had my credit card but that was only accidentally. In the States
getting notarization is often free—at least it always has been
whenever I've needed it.

Thus, I showed up thinking that the same would be the case
at my country's Embassy. Boy was I wrong. When they told me the
price to sign and stamp two pieces of paper, my jaw dropped to the
floor. And when I asked if they would take my credit card and the
response was no, it was like someone tripped over that jaw lying in
the floor. I couldn't believe it.

So, I was standing at the window, talking via a push-button
microphone through a thick piece of bullet-proof glass to an
Embassy representative. I was trying to figure out whether I had any
other options and his only advice was to go to a bank and come
back. Well, time wasn't on my side so that really wasn't an option at
the moment.

Then, all of a sudden, I heard a voice behind me say, "How
much do you need?" I turned around to look and there was Linoy, a
native Ethiopian, sitting in the first row of about six rows waiting for
her turn in line. Because I was a native citizen the Embassy actually

moved me to the front of the line (that made me a little uncomfortable but I was in a hurry so I wasn't arguing). When I made eye contact with her she said it again, "How much do you need?" And then she said, "If they'll take local money, birr, I can probably help you." So, I said, "$100." She didn't hesitate, she didn't think twice about it, and she was eager to help. She opened her purse, pulled out 2,500 birr (just over $100) and handed it to me.

I told her, I don't have my Ethiopian phone on me because they took it at the gate. And I don't' remember the number to it. I thought that might make her change her mind but it didn't. She shrugged and said, "No problem!" (ችግር የለም: chIh-gehr yEh-lehm) I then told her where I was staying and she had never heard of it. I thought for sure that this would cause her to change her mind because things were only sounding more and more suspicious. But it didn't. Again, "No problem!"

Then I asked her to give me her contact information. She wrote it down and handed it to me. At that point, I was just in awe. What an amazing and generous person. I learned a little bit about her story and also shared a bit of mine. I gleaned that she was a native Ethiopian who grew up in Israel and eventually moved to L.A. She moved back to Ethiopia in order to start a business designing and constructing buildings, a business meant to provide many locals with work. That was her goal: to give back to her home country and be a positive influence in the lives of many.

Later that night, once I arrived back at the hotel, I texted her and set up a meeting for the next day to pay her back. Still, she was cool and nonchalant about it. And the next evening, I met her to pay her back. When I did, she invited me and my children to dinner a few nights later. In the midst of being in the city's rat race all day every day, I stopped a bit to dwell on this and the beauty of it. It gives me hope for humanity and hope for Ethiopia. And if you ever happen to read this, Linoy, again, I just want to say, "Thank you!" (አመሰግናለሁ: ah-meh-seh-gih-nAh-leh-hu).

Focal Words: Crazy (እብድ: Ihbd) | Page (ገጽ: gEhts') | No problem! (ችግር የለም: chIh-gehr yEh-lehm) | Thank you! (አመሰግናለሁ: ah-meh-seh-gih-nAh-leh-hu)

Your Turn:

Inmates

Focal Words: Door (በር: bEhr) | They (እነሱ: ih-nEh-su) | Courthouse (ፍርድ ቤት: fIhr-dih bayt) | We (እኛ: Ihn-yah)

If you happen to darken the door (በር: bEhr) of the Federal Court building in Addis Ababa on any given morning, you're likely to see large groups of inmates corralled together on the lower floor. The typical dress is either a red or orange one-piece cloth jumpsuit with a pair of plastic sandals. Oh, and don't forget the jewelry—the silver handcuffs. Each inmate wears one cuff on his wrist and is chained to another prisoner.

Usually, those in bonds are told to sit on the floor. As they (እነሱ: ih-nEh-su) do, they are surrounded by guards. The guards have blue, black, and white camouflage garb on. Their jewelry consists of a knightstick and a rifle or some sort of AK. Because of this, given the numerous times I have seen this morning ritual at the courthouse (ፍርድ ቤት: fIhr-dih bayt), I have never witnessed one person trying anything fishy.

It is quite an odd thing really. These inmates typically arrive on a bus together, which is often pretty tough looking. It has wire-grated windows and looks somewhat similar to what we (እኛ: Ihn-yah) might see in America but just always a bit more used and older looking. Once the bus door opens, it's almost like a ritual. The inmates are paraded, out in public, from the bus to the first floor where they sit until further notified. Sometimes that takes quite a while.

So, while I'm just a few feet away from them waiting for adoption paperwork to be signed, there they are just looking around. They don't seem to talk much, although, that doesn't seem prohibited. But admittedly, it's a little eerie feeling. I'm there trying to open up a future of hope and possibility for children and right next to me are a number of humans facing time behind bars—a future of struggle and little to no possibility.

Sometimes while I'm waiting, I say prayers for these guys.

(There are also women, too, but the number of women I've seen I can basically count on one hand.) I don't know their names, I don't know who they are, I don't know what they've done but I know that I hope there is also a better future ahead for them, whatever their circumstances. Were I in the know about whatever crimes they might have committed, perhaps I wouldn't pray as much or at all. I don't know. But at the end of the day, what stands out most to me is the fact that I'm struck by the profound difference in their being there versus mine, their reasons versus mine. It's like a collision of worlds.

Focal Words: Door (በር: bEhr) | They (እነሱ: ih-nEh-su) | Courthouse (ፍርድ ቤት: fIhr-dih bayt) | We (እኛ: Ihn-yah)

Your Turn:

I Don't Drink Coffee

Focal Words: Chair (ወንበር: wEhn-behr) | Table (ጠረጴዛ: t'eh-reh-p'Ay-zah) | I don't drink __ (አልጠጣም: Ahl-t'eh-t'ahm) | Cup (ሲኒ: sEE-nee) | Spoon (ማንኪያ: mAhn-kee-yah)

One thing I enjoy about coming to Ethiopia is meeting new people. They are everywhere! In Addis Ababa there are millions of new people; well, new-to-me people, anyway. There have really only been two or three times, out of many, that I've felt a bit uncomfortable here. Naturally, I'm just trusting and love getting a chance to practice the language, meet the locals, and learn about the culture.

When I see chances to do those things, I jump on them. One such opportunity arose on a very rainy day while walking down a muddy road to the orphanage where my daughter was. On this particular day the mud was so deep and the road so soaked that a car just couldn't make it. Thus, a friend and I decided to hoof it. Well, on the way, a guy named Anbessa, an Amharic name that means "lion," decided to start walking with us.

He introduced us to his mother, sister, and friends who were around the area. He also invited us into a little shop, not at all far from the orphanage, for coffee. Since I am not a coffee drinker, I didn't want to be rude. So, I obliged and entered into the shop. The friend who was with me, one who had something of a military background, was quite nervous. He was scoping the little shop out and staying on high alert with regard to anything suspicious about to happen. We were, after all, two white guys in a non-descript shack and, in Ethiopia, to most white skin equals an absurd amount of wealth.

Anyway, as I sat down in my chair (ወንበር: wEhn-behr) with my knees butted up against a brown wooden table (ጠረጴዛ: t'eh-reh-p'Ay-zah), Anbessa offered me coffee. My response was, "I don't drink it" (አልጠጣም: Ahl-t'eh-t'ahm). So, I kindly declined the cup (ሲኒ: sEE-nee) but wanted to stick around for the conversation. It wasn't a deep conversation by any stretch of the imagination, but more along the lines of a let's-try-to-get-to-know-one-another-despite-the-language-barrier exchange. As each of the five guys in the shop sat drinking and stirring the coffee in their cups with a spoon (ማንኪያ: mAhn-kee-yah), I seized the opportunity to practice my Amharic. All of them were shocked that I could carry on a bit of a conversation and had a little vocabulary under my belt.

I could tell, however, that my friend was getting highly uncomfortable. So, we took off just a few minutes later. He confirmed that he was, indeed, rather nervous...even to the point of sitting by the exit and being ready for take-off at any moment. It is interesting how our perspectives of that even were so different. He said it was the worst cup of coffee he had ever had. I laughed at that and wondered if some of it had to do with the company we were keeping there, company that seemed to make the moment (and perhaps taste) extra bitter for him. Maybe. Maybe not.

Focal Words: Chair (ወንበር: wEhn-behr) | Table (ጠረጴዛ: t'eh-reh-p'Ay-zah) | I don't drink ___ (አልጠጣም: Ahl-t'eh-t'ahm) | Cup (ሲኒ: sEE-nee) | Spoon (ማንኪያ: mAhn-kee-yah)

Your Turn:

The Daughter That Never Was

Focal Words: Bad (ጥፉ: tIh-fu) | Funny (አስቂኝ: ahs-qEEn-yih) | Smile (ፈገግታ: feh-gEhg-tah)

    When you have a deep drive to see the world orphan crisis end, and when you take seriously the biblical claim that "true" or "pure" region includes looking after orphans, and when you spend week after week and day after day with orphans, you bond with them. Yes, you definitely want to adopt them all or see them all adopted but sometimes there's one that, well, just feels like your own kid. And in spite of all the hoops one has to go through to get a child (or 3) adopted in a place like Ethiopia, something inside you reminds you that you would do it again in a heartbeart. If you could!

    During my recent 2-month stint in Ethiopia, I bonded with many kids in the orphanages my children were in. And aside from my own little ones, there was one young girl, Sara, who just seemed like she was my daughter. I loved this little girl to pieces and even went to the orphanage and government officials to ask about adopting her. Their response was frustrating, but one of the responses I received from an older girl in the orphanage was downright stomach-turning.

    The government replied that she was ineligible for adoption for 2 reasons: 1) Because I was a foreigner and the government is in the process of shutting down international adoption, and 2) About a month ago, her dad showed up and asked for her. They didn't release her to him because she was in school. He had not yet come back again. The thing is, I've talked with Ts'ara and she wouldn't recognize her dad if she saw him. She has been in the orphanage since she was an infant and now she is 10. At some point, however, she learned that he was a Muslim because she's shared that with me on several occasions. The thing is, in 10 years, he's never been to visit her. Not once. Her mom has never been in the picture either.

    When I told one of the older girls at the orphanage the bit

about Ts'ara's dad visiting, she replied, "Oh, that is bad (ጥፉ: tIh-fu)!" I asked her why and she, too, knowing that Ts'ara's dad was a Muslim said, "Because he is only coming back to get her in order to sell her. That's a Muslim tradition. Some put their children in the orphanage until they are old enough to sell them. The government feeds them and raises them and then they are taken. She will become a child bride."

At that, my heart was just crushed. My eyes filled with tears. This is a little girl that I was willing (and still am willing!) to adopt. This is a little girl who feels like she's my own daughter. This is a little girl who is funny (አስቂኝ: ahs-qEEn-yih), smart, and has a one-of-a-kind smile (ፈገግታ: feh-gEhg-tah) that lights up an entire room. This is a little girl who is full of potential that may never be realized because of beurocratic read tape. This is a little girl who, for me, is the daughter that never was. And that reality just kills me. It breaks my heart. I just want better for her. I want her to know what it's like to have a family, to have a loving mother and father, and to sleep in a comfortable bed. Really, I just want all the things for her that I want for my own kids. Because, well, she feels like my kid.

Focal Words: Bad (ጥፉ: tIh-fu) | Funny (አስቂኝ: ahs-qEEn-yih) | Smile (ፈገግታ: feh-gEhg-tah)

Your Turn:

Abdissa

Focal Words: Evening (ማታ: mAh-tah) | Lunch (ምሳ: mIh-sah) | Tradition (ልማድ: lIh-mahd) | Even (እንኳን: Ihn-kwahn) | Because (ስለ: sIh-leh)

From morning 'til evening (ማታ: mAh-tah), I spent much of each day on my recent trip to Ethiopia in a tiny, light blue, 1980s Corolla riding across Addis Ababa. Many days I skipped lunch (ምሳ: mIh-sah) and just clocked hours. Indeed, every day for nearly 2 months I rode with a friend, a local, named Abdissa, who put in lots of effort and long days. He's a Christian of the Ethiopian Orthodox tradition (ልማድ: lIh-mahd), his boss is a Muslim, and in a city filled with many people who don't work, this guy works his tail off. I marvel at his work ethic!

On many days, while I would be biding my time in government buildings, he would be sitting in the car ready and waiting for me to return. Sometimes those waits lasted upwards of 6, 7, and even (እንኳን: Ihn-kwahn) 8 hours. Insane! Yes, I found him napping a few times but I can't blame him at all, I would have done the same if I could have. In fact, there might have been a few days where I was a little bit jealous of him for that.

I write about Abdissa here because (ስለ: sIh-leh), well, this is in part a book about the people, places, and things I encountered throughout Ethiopia. So, how could I not offer up a short bit about the person I likely spent more time with than anyone else?! I couldn't do that. I couldn't do that because this is the guy who, when a street beggar slapped me on the chest with a rag while we were sitting at a stoplight, unbuckled his seatbelt and was ready to chase that guy down in an instant.

This was the guy who rushed me back and forth across the city to pick up paperwork, make it to appointments, see my kids, and lend a hand to others. This is the guy who provided a ride when I was able to take my daughter out to a restaurant for the first time. This is the guy who fielded phone calls in Amharic for me when I couldn't understand. This is the guy who, despite maybe not even realizing it, had one of the biggest roles in helping move my kids' cases along toward their end-goals.

And for those things and many more, I am forever grateful to this guy, my friend. We managed to work together for 2 months despite the language barrier, despite not really knowing each other at first, and despite all the hurdles the adoption process threw at me. Abdissa was there sighing and shaking his head and groaning right along with me when things fell through. No, he wasn't as invested in the process as me, but he was invested nevertheless. And when you go from simply being a cab driver to someone wading into the high weeds of international adoption, that says something about your character.

So, Abdissa, here's to you! And here's a massive "Thank you!" from my family! Thank you for helping us! Thank you for being there for me, for being reliable, and for being an honest guy. Keep doing what you're doing and please realize that what you are doing is not merely driving a taxi. You are helping change kids' lives and helping put families together. This is no insignificant thing at all. In fact, it's a pretty big deal. And you, my friend, you are a pretty big deal. That's the truth.

Focal Words: Evening (ማታ: mAh-tah) | Lunch (ምሳ: mIh-sah) | Tradition (ልማድ: lIh-mahd) | Even (እንኳን: Ihn-kwahn) | Because (ስለ: sIh-leh)

Your Turn:

You Might Be An Ethiopian If...

Focal Words: Breakfast (ቁርስ: qUrs) | Dinner (እራት: ih-rAht) | Yes (አዎ: Ah-woh)

One thing that I really enjoy about Ethiopia is spending time with friends here and getting to joke around with them. Truth be told, when you spend countless hours in the car every day, some comic relief is like a balm to the soul. It's fun when us foreigners and the locals can poke fun at and tease each other. So, it is in that spirit and in the style of comedian, Jeff Foxworthy, that I offer the following "You Might be an Ethiopian if..." jokes.

- You might be an Ethiopian if...showing up 4 hours late seems early to you.
- You might be an Ethiopian if...your job description demands find creative ways to get out of work.
- You might be an Ethiopian if...you charage a skin tax at your shop or to ride in your taxi.
- You might be an Ethiopian if...looking both ways before crossing seems dumb.
- You might be an Ethiopian if...you view pedestrians as moving targets.
- You might be an Ethiopian if...you answer the phone with, "Hello!? Hello!? Hello!? Hello!? Hello!?"
- You might be an Ethiopian if...you eat injera...for breakfast (ቁርስ: qUrs), lunch, and dinner (እራት: ih-rAht).
- You might be an Ethiopian if...your baby turns 1 at 13-months old.
- You might be an Ethiopian if...you get walls confused with urinals.
- You might be an Ethiopian if...you stop working because it's raining.
- You might be an Ethiopian if...you love meetings so much that, when the power goes out, you turn on your phone screen

so you can help keep the party going in the dark.

- You might be an Ethiopian if...you celebrate the network being down because, even though you're in the office, it's another day off work.
- You might be an Ethiopian if...you break out the limp "wristshake" when yout hands are wet.
- You might be an Ethiopian if...you can hear someone saying "Yes!" (አዎ: Ah-woh) just by raising their eyebrows.
- You might be an Ethiopian if...you sound like you're short on breath and gasping for air when agreeing with someone.
- You might be an Ethiopian if...your car is held together by zip ties.

Focal Words: Breakfast (ቁርስ: qUrs) | Dinner (እራት: ih-rAht) | Yes (አዎ: Ah-woh)

Your Turn:

A Bright(on) Spot

Focal Words: Shop (ሱቅ: sUq) | Dress (Traditional) (ሸማ: shEh-mah) | Shirt (Traditional) (ሐበሻ: hAh-beh-shah) | Only (ብቻ: bIh-chah)

As one begins to ascend Mt. Entoto via the Shiro Meda area, they will encounter shop (ሱቅ: sUq) after shop. Most of the tiny stores sell the traditional Ethiopian dress (ሸማ: shEh-mah) for females and the traditional Ethiopian shirt (i.e. Habesha shirt) (ሐበሻ: hAh-beh-shah) for males. One of the interesting things about Ethiopia, well, to me anyway, is that different parts of the city consist of shops that sell the same materials.

In other words, if you need a book, you can go to one area of the city and all the bookstores, selling exactly the same books, are right next door to one another. The same goes for auto parts—all the shops are right next to each other selling the same parts. It's an awful business plan but that's the way it is—Ethiopian business owners just think it's too risky to move a few blocks over. But I digress. Back to Shiro Media.

As you drive past the tiny shops, you have to look closely because you might miss one of the best places in all of Ethiopia: Brighton Academy. It is a private school, one my daughter has attended for over a year, in fact, and last year was the only (ብቻ: bIh-chah) new school to open in the entire city. It already has 150 students and about that many waitlisted.

Here the students learn English, Amharic, math, science, biology, and the like. It is a great school and, as it continues to grow, will provide many young Ethiopians with an opportunity to put their education and knowledge to use rather than letting it fall to the wayside. The children are also fed twice a day, given clean water, and are loved dearly by their teachers.

The school was started in memory and in honor of the founders' son, whom they named Brighton. Several years ago, the family was set to adopt their little boy but before they could finish the process, he passed. Today, however, his legacy and story live on through the many kids who attend this school. And it will continue to live on as these children grow into young adults and use what they learn to make Ethiopia a better, more just place. Think about the possibilities of this place gives me some hope. In a place where many don't value education or don't know the value of it, Brighton stands out as a bright spot on the map. May it continue to shine!

Focal Words: Shop (ሱቅ: sUq) | Dress (Traditional) (ሽማ: shEh-mah) | Shirt (Traditional) (ሐበሻ: hAh-beh-shah) | Only (ብቻ: bIh-chah)

Your Turn:

I've Seen a Lot

Focal Words: Promise / Covenant (ቃል ኪዳን: qAhl kee-dahn) | Patience (ትግስት: tIh-gihst) | Paradise (ገነት: gEh-neht) | Hair (ጸጉር: ts'Eh-gur)

Perhaps it's the linguist in me, perhaps it's just sheer curiousity, or perhaps it's something else, I don't know, but I find names from other cultures fascinating. When I encounter a new name, I love asking whether there is some sort of significance or meaning behind the name.

Some of my favorite Ethiopan names in this regard are "Kalkidan" (ቃል ኪዳን: qAhl kee-dahn) which means "promise" or "covenant," "Tigist" (ትግስት: tIh-gihst), which means "patience," and "Genet" (ገነት: gEh-neht), which means "paradise." A new name that I recently learned of is "Bizu Ayew," which means "I've seen a lot." This was the name of a little girl, probably 8 or 9 years old, whom I met on a day we took a group of kids from the Korah (or: Kore) slum on an all-day trip.

The last stop on our trip that day was a tiny little theme park. We had about 60 kids with us and before they left, they were all waiting in line to get on the ferris wheel. Bizu Ayew was standing near the front of the line and had been for a while. She had black hair (ጸጉር: ts'Eh-gur), just past shoulder length, that was wavy and beautiful.

She wore high-top tennis shoes, black jeans, and a t-shirt. I had been standing there talking with her for several minutes when someone spoke to me so I turned around. In the short amount of time I had turned away and then back, a young boy had tried to cut in front of her. When she tried to stop him, he elbowed her in the face, right in the forehead. So, I turned back only to see her crying and holding her face, not so much like she was in pain, but more like she was in shame.

A male had just hit this young girl in public. One could simply chalk it up to their age, them being kids, but I don't think that's the case at all. This is something that, in my view, starts at a young age like this in culture and then persists. How do I know? Because I've witnessed it with my own eyes. Just a few weeks before, for instance, I saw a grown man hit a young girl in the face.

That guy, named "Antena," was a guard at a government-run orphanage. His name, interestingly, means "that guy." That's right, he's "that guy," the one who used his power to bully a child. He's "that guy," the one who wears an Orthodox cross necklace but hardly sees and treats these orphans how Christ would have. He's "that guy" who, when I confronted him about it, gave me the line, "She's stubborn and deserves it."

What was she being stubborn about? Getting in a group with the rest of the kids to look at the pictures on a cell phone. Yes, that's what earned her a slap in the face from a grown man. A slap that gave her a bruise above her eye and made her feel so embarrassed and ashamed and untrusting of grown men that she wouldn't let me hug her to console her. In my 2 months, I saw this little girl just about every day. She wasn't stubborn at all. She was sweet and kind. But also the victim of an incredibly broken system. Period!

And she, too, was experiencing early on what something she'll likely experience the rest of her life. Her name was not Bizu Ayew, but like her, she could already say at such a young age, "I've seen a lot." Indeed, these kids will truly have seen and experienced some of the worst things the world has to offer and some of the worst things their country has to offer at such a young age. They will have encountered many of life's harshest realities as youngsters, things that most in already-developed countries may never ever have to experience.

Focal Words: Promise / Covenant (ቃል ኪዳን: qAhl kee-dahn) | Patience (ትግስት: tIh-gihst) | Paradise (ገነት: gEh-neht) | Hair (ጸጉር: ts'Eh-gur)

Your Turn:

Fodder for Paper Airplanes

Focal Pages: Place (በታ: bOh-tah) | Long-term (ቆሚ: qwAh-mee) | Room (ክፍል: kih-fIhl) | Number (ቁጥር: qU-tihr)

During a number of my visits to the orphanage, I encountered missionaries who were just passing through for the day. Personally, I am not a fan of short-term missions. Well, I suppose I should qualify that: The only condition in which I support short-term missions is if those going are doing so with the mindset and intent of investing in the people and place (በታ: bOh-tah) they are serving long-term (ቆሚ: qwAh-mee). It is simply a waste of time and money to go to a place like Ethiopa for a week, only to never return or have anything else to do with the place.

I've heard the refrains, "Short-term missions do more good for those going than for those they're going to see." I agree with that statement. And it's because I agree with it that I am also opposed: no mission trip should revolve around me getting to feel sorry for others so that, ultimately, I can feel better about myself and my own situation. Church leaders, trip leaders, and the like, need to come to the realization that when they lead with this mindset, they are simply perpetuating a type of voyeuristic and narcissistic cycle.

What, do we think that people in places like Ethiopia cannot paint a room (ክፍል: kih-fIhl) themselves? Do we in the West really need to be organizing temas to cross the ocean to go paint? Do we really think that when people can't afford to buy food or clothes or have an education, that us painting their shack or the orphanage is what's going to make a difference? Are we that foolish? Seriously, are we?

Don't get me wrong, at one point, I, too, played into this mindset. I'm not just trying to peach to the choir. It's just that now, having seen what happens when one stays for months or years, I can no longer in good conscience support short-term trips unless, as I already said, there's also a long-term element somehow built in.

One of the things I saw on my recent trip, for instance, was a group of about 6 Americans arriving at the orphanage where my daughter was staying. They stayed for maybe 15-20 minutes. What did they do? They got out of their plush van, "toured" the orphanage, felt sorry for the kids, tried to snap a few photos with the little African kids, handed them some alphabet and number (ቁጥር: qU-tihr) workbooks, and when it started to rain they left. That was it.

Want to know what happened to those workbooks in less than 15 minutes after they left? Every single page was ripped out of them. Every! Last! Page! And the kids were bringing the pages to me to make paper airplanes for them. There was no reading, no studying, no writing, none of that. No, they had no interest. Thus, these workbook pages became fodder for paper airplanes.

That little trip those people made to the orphanage that day was pointless. In fact, I tend to think trips like those ultimately do more harm than good. Yes, the foreigners might leave feeling like the've done something good, but we need to ask if they really have. I say, quite emphatically, "No!" As I noted with regard to the Western side of things, it simply keeps a vicious cycle of voyeurism and narcissim alive. And with regard to the kids and the Ethiopian side, it engenders a mentality that seeing a foreign person means handouts are on the way and that they themselves don't need to do anything because foreigners will always come to the rescue.

People may go on short trips to Ethiopia with the best of intentions. This can happen. And, again, if they go with the intent of a long-term investment, I'm all for that. But I also think people really need to question themselves when considering a short-term trip to Ethiopia or anywhere else. An important question to ask is: "Would all the money I'm going to spend to go there fore a week be put to better use if I were to give it to an organization with long-term roots there?" If the answer is "Yes," then one should not go but simply work from wherever they may live to raise support and send it over. Otherwise, it's just a waste of money. It's like throwing money into the air. Or, stated differently, it's like throwing money at children who know no better and, as a result, simply use it, too, for something like paper airplanes.

Focal Pages: Place (በታ: bOh-tah) | Long-term (ቋሚ: qwAh-mee) | Room (ክፍል: kih-fIhl) | Number (ቁጥር: qU-tihr)

Your Turn:

Vocabulary Review #7

Bad (ጥፉ: tIh-fu)
Because (ስለ: sIh-leh)
Breakfast (ቁርስ: qUrs)
Building (ሕንጻ: hIhn-ts'ah)
Chair (ወንበር: wEhn-behr)
Courthouse (ፍርድ ቤት: fIhr-dih bayt)
Crazy (እብድ: Ihbd)
Cup (ሲኒ: sEE-nee)
Dinner (እራት: ih-rAht)
Door (በር: bEhr)
Dress (Traditional) (ሸማ: shEh-mah)
Even (እንኳን: Ihn-kwahn)
Evening (ማታ: mAh-tah)
Face (ፊት: fEEt)
Funny (አስቂኝ: ahs-qEEn-yih)
Hair (ጸጉር: ts'Eh-gur)
I Don't Drink __ (አልጠጣም: Ahl-t'eh-t'ahm) In (በ: bEh)
Long-term (ቋሚ: qwAh-mee)
Lunch (ምሳ: mIh-sah)
No problem! (ችግር የለም: chIh-gehr yEh-lehm) Number (ቁጥር: qU-tihr)
Only (ብቻ: bIh-chah)
Page (ገጽ: gEhts')
Paradise (ገነት: gEh-neht)
Patience (ትግስት: tIh-gihst)
Place (ቦታ: bOh-tah)
Promise / Covenant (ቃል ኪዳን: qAhl kee-dahn) Room (ክፍል: kih-fIhl)
Shirt (Traditional) (ሐበሻ: hAh-beh-shah) Shop (ሱቅ: sUq)
Smile (ፈገግታ: feh-gEhg-tah)
Spoon (ማንኪያ: mAhn-kee-yah)

Table (ጠረጴዛ: t'eh-reh-p'Ay-zah)
Thank you! (አመሰግናለሁ: ah-meh-seh-gih-nAh-leh-hu)
They (እነሱ: ih-nEh-su)
Tradition (ልማድ: lIh-mahd)
Wall (ግድግዳ: gEhd-geh-dah)
We (እኛ: Ihn-yah)
Yes (አዎ: Ah-woh)

Yared & Mengi

Focal Words: Memory (ትዝታ: tIh-zih-tah) | Friendship (ወዳጅነት: weh-dAh-jih-neht) | Both (ሁለቱም: hu-lEh-tum) | My (የኔ: yEh-nay)

As with any international trip, when you're returning to the United States via plane, you will be handed a claims form by U.S. Immigration. They ask you questions like how like you were traveling (they should already know that!), the nature of your travel, and what goods you purchased and are bringing back. On the back of the form they ask you to list those items and their respective values.

Recently, after I finished filling that form out, the thought came to mind that I'm bringing back many intangible things that are worth far more. But, of course, they don't ask about those. Things like a valuable memory (ትዝታ: tIh-zih-tah) or friendship (ወዳጅነት: weh-dAh-jih-neht). With regard to the latter, I want to mention here two friends I made during my 2-month stay in Ethiopia: Yared and Mengi (short for Mengistu). Both guys worked together for an adotion agency and were social workers. And were it not for both (ሁለቱም: hu-lEh-tum) of them, I'm not sure my (የኔ: yEh-nay) son's paperwork would have made it through the system with the haste that it did.

The thing is, I met these guys randomly one day while sitting in a federal government building. I had been sitting there for 5 or 6 hours when they came in. When they arrived, they were able to get their paperwork to move through the system much faster than I could get mine to. That's likely because they were not only winsome, but knew the process and were familiar with the people. Seeing me sitting there, they began talking to me and I shared a bit about my situation.

Right away they strategized to help get my paperwork to the same point as theirs, essentially grouping things together. At one point, however, my paperwork got behind theirs because, as it was getting ready to be signed, a meeting was called. I watched theirs move from one room to the other, a sign denoting progress, while mine got stuck. But Yared wasn't freaking out like I was. His comment was, "We wait here until his paperwork moves, too. We're not leaving today without this guy."

And in that moment, I knew I could absolutely trust these two. Despite the fact that they had their own clients and worked for another adoption agency, they gave up their time and availed their knowledge and relationships to help me and one of my children. But it was not just that day. Mengi, especially, was a big help over the course of the next month. He frequently called to check on me, allowed me to call and text him for advice, and showed me over and over again that he was in it for all the right reasons. Sadly, I can't say that about too many others who have similar roles in other organizations. But when you find a good thing, you need to share it. That's precisely what I'm doing here.

Focal Words: Memory (ትዝታ: tIh-zih-tah) | Friendship (ወዳጅነት: weh-dAh-jih-neht) | Both (ሁለቱም: hu-lEh-tum) | My (የኔ: yEh-nay)

Your Turn:

A Strict Diet

Focal Words: Meat (ሥጋ: sEh-gah) | Potato (ድንች: dIh-nehch) | Fat
(ወፍራም: wEhf-rahm) | Skinny (ከሲት: kEh-seet)

I'm not an adventurous eater. I never have been. I grew up on
a steady diet of meat (ሥጋ: sEh-gah) and potato (ድንች: dIh-nehch)
pretty much every day. Ever since, I have never really ventured too
far from that. Thus, when it comes to eating in Ethiopia, I'm quite
out of my element. Other than the fact that there are actually many
days where busyness takes over and I simply forget to eat, menu-
wise there aren't a lot of options that appeal to me.

Plus, when I have to make every hour of every day count, I
can't afford to try too many new things. So, I play it safe—always.
That's why, out of my 6 times in Ethiopia, I've only been sick once.
That was on this recent trip after I ate chicken at a local restaurant.
From that point on, I pretty much had a steady diet of Sprite, eggs,
and French fries whenever I sat down to eat.

This resulted in me losing 15 pounds, which also resulted in
all of my clothes appearing incredibly baggy on me. In the end, I no
longer looked like a fat (ወፍራም: wEhf-rahm) foreigner, but a skinny
(ከሲት: kEh-seet) foreigner wearing over-sized clothes. And when I
returned back to America, I couldn't even halfway finish my meal.

For 2 months, I basically dreamt about eating an American
hamburger. So, when I landed in the States, during a 5-hour layover,
I went to a restaurant to order one. Much to my surprise, my waitress
was Ethiopian. So, not only did I get to try speaking Amharic with
her, I got to order my burger. When the time came to eat it, however,
my stomach felt like it had shrunk. It seemed like I could feel myself
gaining weight. It tasted great but also felt very heavy about halfway
through.

I don't know if I can keep my steady Ethiopian diet while
here in America, but I kind of want to. Eating once or, at most, twice
a day, seems like a good idea. And it's at least part of the reason why
most Ethiopians just aren't overweight. When I was talking to my

waitress, in fact, about losing so much weight, she said, "In Ethiopia we don't really know fat Ethiopians. We don't really have them." That's quite true; they are few and far between. And maybe for Westerners it's something worth paying attention to.

Focal Words: Meat (ሥጋ: sEh-gah) | Potato (ድንች: dIh-nehch) | Fat (ወፍራም: wEhf-rahm) | Skinny (ከሲት: kEh-seet)

Your Turn:

From Japan with Love

Focal Words: Soccer (የእግር ኳስ: yEh-gihr qwahs) | Bridge (ድልድይ: dIhl-diy) | Her (የርሷ: yEhr-swah) | Them (እነሱን: ih-nEh-sun)

It's something of a rarity to find someone from Japan in Ethiopia. The same is not true of persons from China. The presence of China is felt all over Ethiopia. China has invested in road-building, is constructing the new soccer (የእግር ኳስ: yEh-gihr qwahs) stadium, has given the country the newly-built African Embassy, and has major projects underway in many corners of Ethiopia.

As I said, however, the presence of Japan is not all that evident. I was surprised that in the Blue Nile basin, however, that there is a new bridge (ድልድይ: dIhl-diy) that crosses the river and it was a Japan-based project. But during my time in Ethiopia, I met a Japanese woman named Sayuri. She was a friend of a friend with tons of vision, courage, and most importantly, love.

She was in Addis at the same time I was but with a different agenda. Sayuri was in the initial phase of launching an NGO (Non-governmental Organization) aiming to remove women from the viscious web of prostitution. Or, stated differently, her (የርሷ: yEhr-swah) goal was to rescue women forced by economics or other factors, into the sex-for-sale trade. As she explained her goals, I couldn't help but marvel.

At the same time, after I got to know her, I wasn't at all surprised. This, after all, was a woman who knew neither me nor my friend yet went with us 3 hours outside of Addis to go hiking in a nondescript location with a makeshift tour guide. And this was the woman who spent another weekend with us when we took 60 kids out to the countryside and to the theme park. She packed into the bus with them (እነሱን: ih-nEh-sun) and, despite the Japanese-Amharic language barrier, showed them the love of Christ all day long.

As far as I understood her story, Sayuri is the only Christian in her family. This, at times, has proven to be a struggle for her; nevertheless, she remains faithful. Her smile is infectious, and her kind words are life-giving. But these, along with her demeanor and actions ultimately tell less about her and more about the God she loves and serves. That's a rare thing to encounter but precisely what is needed in the hard line of work she now finds herself in.

Focal Words: Soccer (የእግር ካስ: yEh-gihr qwahs) | Bridge (ድልድይ: dIhl-diy) | Her (የርሷ: yEhr-swah) | Them (እነሱን: ih-nEh-sun)

Your Turn:

Beware of the Beembee

Focal Words: BeemBee (ቢምቢ: bEEm-bee) | Ceiling (ጣሪያ: t'Ah-ree-yah | Night (ሌሊት: lAy-leet) | Body (አካል: Ah-kahl) | First (አንደኛ: ahn-dEh-nyah)

In Ethiopa there's a mosquito-like bug that, during the day, tends to stay pretty well hidden. The name of this annoying little creature, which comes out at night and leaves you a few morning presents in the form of red welts, is Beembee (ቢምቢ: bEEm-bee). As far as I know, these bugs carry nothing infectious. I've been the victim of many a Beembee bite with no side affects.

Many of the places I've stayed in Ethiopia, whether guest houses or hotels, have Beembee's around. Moreover, most of these places have portions of their remains smashed on walls, the door, and the ceiling (ጣሪያ: t'Ah-ree-yah). In the most recent place I stayed, there was a Beembee smashed on the ceiling and surrounding it was a black outline of the bottom of a shoe.

Thanks to these little guys, at night (ሌሊት: lAy-leet) I at least start with my entire body (አካል: Ah-kahl) under the covers. Yet, as is typical, I tend to toss and turn out of that position throughout the night. That's when I open myself up to attack. These little critters seem to know it and wait ever so patiently. On my first (አንደኛ: ahn-dEh-nyah) night there this time around, in fact, I woke up only to find a big red bump right below my eye on my cheek bone.

Since the bumps sometimes stay 5 or 6 days, I went nearly a week with this welt on my face. Numerous times while trying to sleep I would hear a Beembee fly up to me. The buzz sound resembles that of a fly or bee. Often, that would lead to the poor little Beembee's demise becuause I would quickly flip the light on and go on the attack. Nothing like standing in your underwear at 3am holding a flip flop in one hand while hunting down a Beembee.

But boy is the victory sweet when you finally get one of them. It frees you up to get back to sleep, to rest a bit easier, and to not have to wake up anymore. But there is an art form to it. These little guys are fast, so, when you go to smack them, you have to be in stealth mode; you have to have precision. If you're ever in Ethiopia, keep an eye out for these critters, especially at night; otherwise, you might just be walking around with a red-welted body.

Focal Words: BeemBee (ቢምቢ: bEEm-bee) | Ceiling (ጣሪያ: t'Ah-ree-yah | Night (ሌሊት: lAy-leet) | Body (አካል: Ah-kahl) | First (አንደኛ: ahn-dEh-nyah)

Your Turn:

Vocabulary Review #8

BeemBee (ቢምቢ: bEEm-bee)
Body (አካል: Ah-kahl)
Both (ሁለቱም: hu-lEh-tum)
Bridge (ድልድይ: dIhl-diy)
Ceiling (ጣሪያ: t'Ah-ree-yah)
Fat (ወፍራም: wEhf-rahm)
First (አንደኛ: ahn-dEh-nyah)
Friendship (ወዳጅነት: weh-dAh-jih-neht)
Her (የርሷ: yEhr-swah)
Meat (ሥጋ: sEh-gah)
Memory (ትዝታ: tIh-zih-tah)
My (የኔ: yEh-nay)
Night (ሌሊት: lAy-leet)
Potato (ድንች: dIh-nehch)
Skinny (ከሲት: kEh-seet)
Soccer (የእግር ኳስ: yEh-gihr qwahs)
Them (እነሱን: ih-nEh-sun)

Bonus Vocabulary Review (#9):
25 More New Words You Already Know

Note: For some of these terms that are alternative words. Those listed here, however, are in common use and, in some instances, have replaced older and/or alternative terms (not listed here).

Africa (አፍሪቃ: ah-frEE-kah)
Aluminum (አሉሚኒየም: ah-lu-mEEn-yem)
Bicycle (ሳይክል: sAy-kehl)
Bus (አውቶቡስ: ahw-tOh-bus)
Camera (ካሜራ: kah-mEh-rah)
Chocolate (ቸኮሌት: chah-koh-lAyt)
Desk (ዴስክ: dAysk)
Fabricate (i.e. make) (ፈብረከ: feh-bEh-reh-keh)
General (ጄኔራል: jAy-nay-rahl)
Grade (in school) (ማርክ: mAhrk)
Internet (ኢንተርኔት: EEn-tehr-nayt)
Islam (እስልምና: ihs-lih-mIh-nah)
Israel (እሥራኤል: ihs-rAh-ayl)
Italy (ጣሊያን: t'Ah-lee-yahn)
Jerusalem (ኢየሩሳሌም: ih-yeh-rU-sah-laym)
Kenya (ኬንያ: kAyn-yah)
Mexico (ሜክሲኮ: mAyk-see-koh)
Motel (ሞተል: mOh-tehl)
Mosque (መስጊድ: mEhs-geed)
Nothing (ምንም: mIh-nih-may)
Nurse (ነርስ: nEhrs)
Pentecostal (ጰንጤ: p'Ehn-t'ay)
Protestant (ፕሮቴስታንት: proh-tays-tAhnt)
Sandwich (ሳንዱች: sAhn-duch)
Siri (ሲሪ: sEE-ree)

Index: Vocabulary Words

(Words marked with * are not used in the book but provided here because they are closely-related and commonly-used.)

Academy (አካዳሚ: ah-kAh-dah-mee)

Acid (አሲድ: Ah-seed)

Adoption (ጉዲፈቻ: gu-di-fAh-chah)

Africa (አፍሪቃ: ah-frEE-kah)

Again (እንደገና: ihn-dEh-geh-nah)

Airplane (አውሮፕላን: ahw-rOhp-lahn)
  *Sometimes spelled (አይሮፕላን: ayih-rOph-lahn)

All Day (ሙሉ ቀን: mU-lu qehn)

Alphabet (ፊደል: fEE-dehl)

Aluminum (አሉሚንየም: ah-lu-mEEn-yem)

Amen (አሜን: Ah-mayn)

America (አሜሪካ: ah-mEh-ree-kah)

Amharic (አማርኛ: ah-mah-rEEn-yah)

And (እና: Ih-nah)

Arcade (አርኬድ: Ahr-kayd)

Backpack (የጉዞ ቦርሳ: yEh-gu-zoh bOhr-sah)

Bad (ጥፉ: tIh-fu)

Ball (ኳስ: kwAhs)

Banana (ሙዝ: mUz)

Bank (ባንክ: bAhnk)

Battery (ባትሪ: bAht-ree) – this can also mean "flashlight" in Amharic

Beautiful (ቆንጆ: qOhn-joh)

Because (ስለ: sIh-leh)

Bedroom (መኝታ ቤት: mehn-yEh-tah bayt)

BeemBee (ቢምቢ: bEEm-bee)

Beer (ቢራ: bEE-rah)

Bible (መጽሐፍ ቅዱስ: mEts'-haf qih-dUs)

Bicycle (ሳይከል: sAy-kehl)

Black (ጥቁር: t'Ih-qur)

Body (አካል: Ah-kahl)

Book (መጽሐፍ: mEhts-haf)

Both (ሁለቱም: hu-lEh-tum)

Boy (ወንድ ልጅ: wEhnd lihj)

Bravo! (ብራቮ: brAh-woh)

Breakfast (ቁርስ: qUrs)

Bridge (ድልድይ: dIhl-diy)

Building (ሕንጻ: hIhn-ts'ah)

Bus (አውቶቡስ: ahw-tOh-bus)

Café (ካፌ: kAh-fay)

Cake (ኬክ: kAyk)

Camera (ካሜራ: kah-mEh-rah)

Candy (ከረሜላ: kah-rah-mAy-lah)

Car (መኪና: meh-kEE-nah)

Ceiling (ጣሪያ: t'Ah-ree-yah)

Chair (ወንበር: wEhn-behr)

Chicken (ዶሮ: dOh-roh)

Children (ልጆች: lee-jOh-ch)

   *Child (ልጅ: lEEj)

Chocolate (ቾኮሌት: chah-koh-lAyt)

Christian (ክርስቲያን: krIhs-tee-yahn)

Ciao (ቻው: chAhw)

Cigar (ሲጋራ: see-gAh-rah) – or cigarette

Cinema (ሲኒማ: sEE-nee-mah)

City (ከተማ: keh-tEh-mah)

Clinic (ክሊኒክ: klEE-neek)

Coat (ኮት: kOht)

Coca-Cola (ኮካ ኮላ: kOh-kah kOh-lah)

Coffee (ቡና: bU-nah)

College (ኮሌጅ: kOh-lehj)

Computer (ኮምፒውተር: kohm-pEEw-tehr)

Condom (ኮንዶም: kOhn-dohm)

Countryside (ባላገር: bah-lAh-gehr)

Courthouse (ፍርድ ቤት: fIhr-dih bayt)

Covenant: *See entry for* "Promise"

Crazy (አብድ: Ihbd)

Cup (ሲኒ: sEE-nee)

Dad / Father (አባባ: ah-bAh-bah)

Daughter (ሴት ልጅ: sAyt lihj)

Day (ቀን: qEhn)

Desk (ዴስክ: dAysk)

Dinner (እራት: ih-rAht)

Diploma (ዲፕሎማ: deep-lOh-mah)

Doctor (ዶክተር: dOhk-tehr)

   *Doctor (ሐኪም: hAh-keem)

Door (በር: bEhr)

Dress (Traditional) (ሸማ: shEh-mah)

Embassy (ኤምባሲ: Aym-bah-see)

English (እንግሊዝኛ: ihng-lee-zIhn-yah)

Ethiopia (ኢትዮጵያ: eet-yO-pee-ya)

Ethiopian (ሐበሻ: hAh-beh-shah)

Even (እንኳን: Ihn-kwahn)

Evening (ማታ: mAh-tah)

Eye (ዐይን: Ah-yihn)

Fabricate (i.e. make) (ፈበረከ: feh-bEh-reh-keh)

Face (ፊት: fEEt)

Family (ቤተሰብ: bay-teh-sEhb)

Fanta (ፋንታ: fAhn-tah)

Far (ሩቅ: rUq)

Fat (ወፍራም: wEhf-rahm)

Film (ፊልም: fEElm)

First (አንደኛ: ahn-dEh-nyah)

Food (ምግብ: mAh-gihb)

Foot (እግር: Ih-gihr)

Foreigner (White person) (ፈረንጅ: feh-rIhnj)

Friend (ጓደኛ: gwah-dEh-nyah)

Friendship (ወዳጅነት: weh-dAh-jih-neht)

Funny (አስቂኝ: ahs-qEEn-yih)

Game (ጨዋታ: ch'Eh-wah-tah)

Garbage Dump (ቆሻ: qOh-shay)

Gate (መዝጊያ: mEhz-gee-yah)

General (ጄኔራል: jAy-nay-rahl)

Give! (ስጠኝ: sih-t'Ehn)

God (እግዚአብሔር: ig-zAhb-heyr)

Government (መንግሥት: mEhn-gihst)

Grade (in school) (ማርክ: mAhrk)

Guard (ዘበኛ: zeh-bEh-nyah)

Hair (ጸጉር: ts'Eh-gur)

Hallelujah (ሃሌሉያ: hah-lay-lU-yah)

Happy (ደስተኛ: dEhs-teh-nyah)

Head (ራስ: rAhs)

Hello (አሎ: Ah-low) – especially when answering phone

Her (የርሷ: yEhr-swah)

Hospital (ሆስፒታል: hos-pEE-tahl)

Hotel (ሆቴል: hOh-tehl)

Hour (ሰዓት: seh-Aht)

I (እኔ: Ih-nee)

I Don't Drink __ (አልጠጣም: Ahl-t'eh-t'ahm)

I Love You! (እወድሻለው: ih-weh-dih-shAh-low) (to a female)

 *I Love You! (እወዳለው: ih-weh-dAh-low) (to a male)

In (በ: bEh)

Injera (እንጀራ: in-jEh-rah)

Internet (ኢንተርኔት: EEn-tehr-nayt)

Islam (እስልምና: ihs-lih-mIh-nah)

Israel (እሥራኤል: ihs-rAh-ayl)

Italy (ጣሊያን: t'Ah-lee-yahn)

Jacket (ጃኬት: jAh-kiht)

Jerusalem (ኢየሩሳሌም: ih-yeh-rU-sah-laym)

Jesus Christ (ኢየሱስ ክርስቶስ: ee-yay-sUs krEEs-tohs)

Job (ሥራ: she-rah)

Kenya (ኬንያ: kAyn-yah)

Kid (ሕፃን: hEh-ts'ahn)

Kilogram (ኪሎ: kEE-loh)

Language (ቋንቋ: kwAhn-kwah)

Leg (እግር: Ih-gihr)

Letter (ደብዳቤ: dehb-dAh-bay)

Lion (አንበሳ: ahn-bEh-sah)

Long-term (ቋሚ: qwAh-mee)
Lunch (ምሳ: mIh-sah)
Man (ወንድ: wEhnd)
Mango (ማንጎ: mAhn-goh)
Many (ብዙ: bIh-zu)
Meat (ሥጋ: sEh-gah)
Memory (ትዝታ: tIh-zih-tah)
Mexico (ሜክሲኮ: mAyk-see-koh)
Million (ሚሊዮን: mEE-lee-yohn)
Minister (ሚኒስትር: mIh-nih-stirh)
Minutes (ደቂቃ: dEh-qee-qah)
Mobile (Cell) Phone (ሞባይል: mOh-bah-yihl)
Money (ብር: bIrr)
Month (ወር: wEhr)
Morning (ጠዋት: t'Eh-waht)
Mosque (መስጊድ: mEhs-geed)
Motel (ሞቴል: mOh-tehl)
Mother (እናት: Ih-naht)
Mouth (አፍ: Ahf)
Mud (ጭቃ: chIh'qah)
Music (ሙዚቃ: mU-zee-qah)
Muslim (ሙስሊም: mUs-leem)
My (የኔ: yEh-nay)
Name (ስም: sIhm)
New (አዲስ: Ah-dees)
Next Day (በማግስቱ: beh-mAh-gihs-tu)
Night (ሌሊት: lAy-leet)
No! (አይ: Aye)
No problem! (ችግር የለም: chIh-gehr yEh-lehm)
North (ሰሜን: sEh-mayn)
Nothing (ምንም: mIh-nih-may)
Number (ቁጥር: qU-tihr)
Nurse (ነርስ: nEhrs)
Office (ቢሮ: bEE-roh) – think "bureau"
Only (ብቻ: bIh-chah)

Or (ወይስ: wEhys)
Page (ገጽ: gEhts')
Pants (ሱሪ: sU-ree)
Papaya (ፓፓያ: pah-pAh-yah)
Paperwork (ወረቀት: weh-reh-qEht)
Paradise (ገነት: gEh-neht)
Park (መናፈሻ: meh-nAh-feh-shah)
Patience (ትግስት: tIh-gihst)
Pen (እስክሪብቶ: is-krEEb-toh)
Pentecostal (ጸንጤ: p'Ehn-t'ay)
People (ሕዝብ: hIh-zihb)
Pepsi (ፐፕሲ: pEhp-see)
Photo (ፎቶ: fOh-toh)
Pizza (ፒዛ: pEE-zah)
Place (ቦታ: bOh-tah)
Police (ፖሊስ: po-lEEs)
Politics (ፖለቲካ: poh-lEh-tee-kah)
Post (ፖስታ: pOhs-tah) – as in "mail"
Potato (ድንች: dIh-nehch)
President (ፕሬዚዳንት: prAy-zee-dahnt)
Printer (ፕሪንተር: prEEn-tehr) – refers to a machine, not a person
Promise (ቃል ኪዳን: qAhl kee-dahn)
Protestant (ፕሮቴስታንት: proh-tays-tAhnt)
Question (ጥያቄ: t'ih-yah-qAy)
Radio (ራዲዮ: rAh-dee-yoh)
Rain (ዝናብ: zEh-nahb)
Rainy Season (ክረምት: keh-rImt)
  *Or: Winter
Restroom (ሽንት ቤት: shIhn-tih-bayt)
River (ወንዝ: wEhnz)
Road (መንገድ: mEhn-gehd)
Rock (ድንጋይ: dIhn-gah-yeh)
Room (ክፍል: kih-fIhl)
Roundabout (አደባባይ: ah-deh-bAh-bay)
Salon (ሳሎን: sah-lOhn)

Sandwich (ሳንዱች: sAhn-duch)

Saturday (ቅዳሜ: qih-dAh-may)

School (ትምህርት: tihm-AIrt)

Science (ሳይንስ: sAh-yihns)

Second (ሁለተኛ: hu-lEh-teh-nyah)

She (እሷ: Ihs-wah)

Shirt (ሸሚዝ: sheh-mEEz)

Shirt (Traditional) (ሐበሻ: hAh-beh-shah)

Shoes (ጫማ: ch'Ah-mah)

Shoestring (የጫማ ማሰሪያ: yeh-chAh-mah mah-sEh-ree-yah)

Shop (ሱቅ: sUq)

Signature (ፊርማ: fIh-rih-mah)

Siri (ሲሪ: sEE-ree)

Sister (እህት: ih-hEht)

Skinny (ከሲት: kEh-seet)

Smart (ጎበዝ: gOh-behz)

Smile (ፈገግታ: feh-gEhg-tah)

Soccer (የእግር ኳስ: yEh-gihr qwahs)

Sofa (ሶፋ: sOh-fah)

Soft Tissue (ሶፍት: sOhft)

Song (ዘፈን: zEh-fehn)

Spoon (ማንኪያ: mAhn-kee-yah)

Sport (ስፖርት: spOhrt)

Sprite (ስፕራይት: SprAh-yiht)

Stapler (ስቴፕለር: stAyp-lehr)

Sugar (ስኳር: sIhw-kahr)

Sun (ፀሐይ: ts'eh-hAh-yih)

Table (ጠረጴዛ: t'eh-reh-p'Ay-zah)

Taxi (ታክሲ: tAhk-see)

Teacher (አስተማሪ: ahs-teh-mAh-ree)

Television (ቴሌቪዥን: tAy-lay-vee-zhihn)

Thank you! (አመሰግናለሁ: ah-meh-seh-gih-nAh-leh-hu)

The (ዜ: zEE)

There (እዚያ: Ihz-yah)

Them (እነሱን: ih-nEh-sun)

They (እነሱ: ih-nEh-su)
Time (ጊዜ: gEE-zay)
Tomorrow (ነገ: nEh-geh)
Tradition (ልማድ: lIh-mahd)
Traditional Ethiopian House (ጎጆ ቤት: gOh-joh bayt)
Truck (ካሚዮን: kAh-mee-yohn)
Upset Stomach (የሆድ መታወክ: ye-hOd meh-tAh-wehk)
Visa (ቪዛ: vEE-zah)
Wall (ግድግዳ: gEhd-geh-dah)
Water (ውሃ: wU-ha)
We (እኛ: Ihn-yah)
Week (ሳምንት: sah-mIhnt)
Weekend (የሳምንት መጨረሻ: yeh-sAh-mihnt meh-chEh-reh-shah)
White (ነጭ: nEhch')
Wife (ሚስት: mEEst)
Window (መስኮት: mEhs-koht)
Winter: See "Rainy Season"
Word (ቃል: qAhl)
World (ዓለም: Ah-lehm)
Year (ዓመት: Ah-meht)
Yes (አዎ: Ah-woh)
Yesterday (ተናንት: tEh-nahnt)
You (አንተ: Ahn-teh) (for a male)
  *You (አንቺ: Ahn-chee) (for a female)
Zipper (ዚፕ: zEEp)

Amharic Alphabet & Pronunciation Guide

Amharic Fidel with Narrow English Transliteration

1	2	3	4	5	6	7
ሀ - ha	ሁ - hu	ሂ - hī	ሃ - haa	ሄ - hā	ህ - hi	ሆ - hō
ለ - la	ሉ - lu	ሊ - lī	ላ - laa	ሌ - lā	ል - li	ሎ - lō
ሐ - ha	ሑ - hu	ሒ - hī	ሓ - haa	ሔ - hā	ሕ - hi	ሖ - hō
መ - me	ሙ - mu	ሚ - mī	ማ - maa	ሜ - mā	ም - mi	ሞ - mō
ሠ - se	ሡ - su	ሢ - sī	ሣ - saa	ሤ - sā	ሥ - si	ሦ - sō
ረ - re	ሩ - ru	ሪ - rī	ራ - raa	ሬ - rā	ር - ri	ሮ - rō
ሰ - se	ሱ - su	ሲ - sī	ሳ - saa	ሴ - sā	ስ - si	ሶ - sō
ሸ - she	ሹ - shu	ሺ - shī	ሻ - shaa	ሼ - shā	ሽ - shi	ሾ - shō
ቀ - qe	ቁ - qu	ቂ - qī	ቃ - qaa	ቄ - qā	ቅ - qi	ቆ - qō
በ - be	ቡ - bu	ቢ - bī	ባ - baa	ቤ - bā	ብ - bi	ቦ - bō
ተ - te	ቱ - tu	ቲ - tī	ታ - taa	ቴ - tā	ት - ti	ቶ - tō
ቸ - che	ቹ - chu	ቺ - chī	ቻ - chaa	ቼ - chā	ች - chi	ቾ - chō
ኀ - he	ኁ - hu	ኂ - hī	ኃ - haa	ኄ - hā	ኅ - hi	ኆ - hō
ነ - ne	ኑ - nu	ኒ - nī	ና - naa	ኔ - nā	ን - ni	ኖ - nō
ኘ - ñe	ኙ - ñu	ኚ - ñī	ኛ - ñaa	ኜ - ñā	ኝ - ñi	ኞ - ñō
አ - a	ኡ - u	ኢ - ī	ኣ - aa	ኤ - ā	እ - i	ኦ - ō
ከ - ka	ኩ - ku	ኪ - kī	ካ - kaa	ኬ - kā	ክ - ki	ኮ - kō
ኸ - kha	ኹ - khu	ኺ - khī	ኻ - khaa	ኼ - khā	ኽ - khi	ኾ - khō
ወ - we	ዉ - wu	ዊ - wī	ዋ - waa	ዌ - wā	ው - wi	ዎ - wō
ዐ - a	ዑ - u	ዒ - ī	ዓ - aa	ዔ - ā	ዕ - i	ዖ - ō
ዘ - ze	ዙ - zu	ዚ - zī	ዛ - zaa	ዜ - zā	ዝ - zi	ዞ - zō
ዠ - zhe	ዡ - zhu	ዢ - zhī	ዣ - zhaa	ዤ - zhāy	ዥ - zhi	ዦ - zhō
የ - ye	ዩ - yu	ዪ - yī	ያ - yaa	ዬ - yā	ይ - yi	ዮ - yō
ደ - de	ዱ - du	ዲ - dī	ዳ - daa	ዴ - dā	ድ - di	ዶ - dō
ጀ - je	ጁ - ju	ጂ - jī	ጃ - jaa	ጄ - jā	ጅ - ji	ጆ - jō
ገ - ge	ጉ - gu	ጊ - gī	ጋ - gaa	ጌ - gā	ግ - gi	ጎ - gō
ጠ - t'e	ጡ - t'u	ጢ - t'ī	ጣ - t'aa	ጤ - t'ā	ጥ - t'i	ጦ - t'ō
ጨ - ch'e	ጩ - ch'u	ጪ - ch'ī	ጫ - ch'aa	ጬ - ch'ā	ጭ - ch'i	ጮ - ch'ō
ጰ - p'e	ጱ - p'u	ጲ - p'ī	ጳ - p'aa	ጴ - p'ā	ጵ - p'i	ጶ - p'ō
ጸ - ts'e	ጹ - ts'u	ጺ - ts'ī	ጻ - ts'aa	ጼ - ts'ā	ጽ - ts'i	ጾ - ts'ō
ፀ - ts'e	ፁ - ts'u	ፂ - ts'ī	ፃ - ts'aa	ፄ - ts'ā	ፅ - ts'i	ፆ - ts'ō
ፈ - fe	ፉ - fu	ፊ - fī	ፋ - faa	ፌ - fā	ፍ - fi	ፎ - fō
ፐ - pe	ፑ - pu	ፒ - pī	ፓ - paa	ፔ - pā	ፕ - pi	ፖ - pō

www.ingramcontent.com/pod-product-compliance
Lightning Source LLC
Chambersburg PA
CBHW060210070426
42447CB00035B/2890